Mega Man 3

Mega Man 3

Salvatore Pane

Boss Fight Books
Los Angeles, CA
bossfightbooks.com

ISBN 13: 978-1-940535-14-2
First Printing: 2016

Series Editor: Gabe Durham
Book Design by Ken Baumann
Page Design by Christopher Moyer

For Theresa

CONTENTS

PROLOGUE

I DIDN'T ASK FOR IT. I didn't even know what it was. All I knew about video games was that my parents owned an Atari 2600 they played religiously—especially *Lost Luggage*, a blocky mess about airport drudgery that didn't appeal to me in the least. It was something for adults, like beer or *Murphy Brown*. But then, on Christmas morning, 1989, I dashed into our living room and discovered a brand new Nintendo Entertainment System under the tree. I was five years old and had no idea how much my life was about to change.

The box immediately set this gift apart from my legion of action figures or board games that featured grinning cartoons. The NES arrived in black and blue cardboard dappled by the blinking stars of outer space. In the center floated an image of the monolithic system itself, boxy and gray, more like a VCR than anything intended for a child, a warp zone to a serious adult world that still valued play. I was mesmerized by the pixelated figure of Mario leaping across a pit of lava in the box's corner and literally trembled with anticipation as my father carefully read the directions and plugged the machine into our console television—complete with faux-wood paneling and cabinet doors. He slid in *Super Mario Bros./Duck Hunt*, and within mere moments we realized just how far we'd come from *Lost Luggage*. Unlike the characters of nearly every Atari game we played, Mario wasn't caged by the walls of our television. The screen scrolled right, into a fully realized world. We didn't understand it then—surely the first level just kept looping—but the promise implied by the NES's box art would be fulfilled. This machine we'd willingly brought into our home contained galaxies.

When my father turned off the NES that night, I cried. Even though I'd played Atari, I assumed that when he pressed power, the game would be erased, that something as powerful and escapist as *Super Mario Bros.* couldn't be accessed anytime we wanted. My parents reassured me, and the next morning I continued my journey, and then on the next and next and next as well.

I remember that Christmas whenever I enter my office as an adult and see firsthand the chaos wrought by that long missing first console. I'm thirty-one. I'm married. I'm an assistant professor of English with specializations in creative writing and digital humanities. I've published a novel. But if you walk into my home office, you won't know any of these things. You will see shelf after shelf of yellowed NES cartridges, over 480 and rising. You will see Famicom games and TurboGrafx-16 HuCards, Sega Saturn discs and PS2 cases, a dusty Apple Macintosh. My television is a dying man on life support, surrounded by surge protectors with literally dozens of cords feeding in from obscure systems ranging from the Magnavox Odyssey 3000 to the Intellivision II, complete with haunting voice module.

Enter my office and you'll sense my hunger to return to that Christmas so long ago.

I

MEGA MAN 2 BEGINS WITH A CUTSCENE, a digital cityscape pierced by a towering, razor-like skyscraper against a jet-black sky. The camera pans up, the music escalating in intensity. Text across the bottom of the screen explains the setting and character motivations: "In the year of 200X, a super robot named Megaman was created. Dr. Light created Megaman to stop the evil desires of Dr. Wily. However, after his defeat, Dr. Wily created eight of his own robots to counter Megaman." Then, the music hits a techno crescendo and we witness our hero standing on a roof, helmet off, hair blowing in the wind like a digital savior. It's one of the most famous introductions to any video game, and for good reason. *Mega Man 2*, released in Japan in 1988, was one of the first console games of its era that didn't just toss you into the fray à la *Super Mario Bros.*

So, you might be surprised the first time you boot up 1990's *Mega Man 3* and observe the comparatively spartan title screen—just the name of the game and two options, Game Start and Password—and hear a slow, downbeat melody. Twenty-four seconds pass before the song kicks into the kind of fast-paced chip music the NES is famous for, but that initial half-minute doesn't at all resemble the bombast and narrative innovation of its more beloved predecessor. *Mega Man 2* is the series's acknowledged masterpiece, and even by the development team's estimation, the follow-up isn't as successful. *Mega Man 3* is the rushed-to-shelves little brother, and the opening reflects that. The title theme is regretful, the lack of a cutscene self-defeating.

Then why does a vocal minority of the fanbase regard *Mega Man 3* as the series's definitive entry? Why is it that when deciding which Mega Man game to cover for this book, I never even considered *Mega Man 2*? Researching the history behind the series and playing *Mega Man 3* over and over again only strengthened my sense that *Mega Man 3* is the apex of its first NES trilogy, the moment when it transitioned from two great games emerging from a mostly singular vision into a full-fledged franchise for Capcom to trot out year after year.

•

After the 1983 video game crash wiped out the majority of American development studios, Japan experienced a digital renaissance led by Nintendo and smaller companies like Konami, Hudson Soft, and Namco. Arcade developer Capcom cultivated a small following on the Famicom—the Japanese equivalent of the NES—by porting its most popular arcade titles like *Commando*, *Ghosts 'n Goblins*, and *1942*, or developing licensed properties from manga and film. But in 1987, the company allowed a lone development team to focus on original software targeted at the growing home console market. Six employees were reassigned, 22-year-old recent college grad Keiji Inafune among them.

Hailing from the city of Kishiwada in the Osaka Prefecture, the fresh-faced Inafune would eventually go on to become the public face of the Mega Man series—much like Shigeru Miyamoto with Super Mario or Hideo Kojima with Metal Gear. But in a 2014 interview in *The Untold History of Japanese Game Developers Volume 1* with J.W. Szczepaniak, Inafune revealed that at the start of his career, he wasn't even interested in game development. "I actually got my first job at Capcom through my artistic desire, through art related job hunting," Inafune said. "It wasn't until *Mega Man* was done and I had worked on it, that I really became interested in game development and creating games. Certainly, my interest when I was growing up was art." A common misconception in America is that Inafune was the lead planner for the original *Mega Man*, but in fact, Capcom tapped Akira Kitamura, a veteran designer who had by that point already worked on Capcom classics *Section Z* and *Legendary Wings*.

Little is known about Kitamura's personal life beyond his fierce desire for privacy, a wish his co-workers still fight to honor decades after his exodus from the games industry in the 90s. But by the time Inafune joined the *Mega Man* development team, the outline for the game and the titular character's pixel sprite had already been completed by Kitamura. Inafune was, however, responsible for drawing Mega Man's animations, including his iconic jump and his running and shooting sprites. In Japan, Kitamura is often referred to as Mega Man's biological father, while Inafune is portrayed as the adoptive father who raised him. When asked by Szczepaniak to describe the working conditions under Kitamura, Inafune said:

> He was an incredibly strict person [...]. He was always in the office, slept at his desk, and he was always researching or working on the games. He taught me about the required strictness of game development. You can't slack off. You have to do your best all the time [...]. Kitamura-san would

sleep through the night, at his desk, and then the next morning he would do the checks for the content that I had produced the day before. Obviously, he didn't sleep so well, and since he was a very, very strict person, often some of the stuff that was good—the stuff that we had all worked on—he would say, "This is no good, and this is no good," and so on. You could say he was a perfectionist. He was incredibly hard to please, with incredibly high standards, and his rules toward character development were so obsessively careful, true perfectionism. That bled over into his approach to game development as a whole. My team in particular really bore the brunt of his drive I guess, his demand for perfection, and we were directly under him [...]. He taught me about the concept of getting exactly what you want for the character onto paper and into the game, not settling merely for something close to your design [...]. He taught me that. I would say that I think the way he taught me, that very strict way, is what kept me interested, and kept me going. Even after he stopped, and I worked on the games without him, I do believe his influence and his approach, which I now believe in, shines through all the products I've worked on, and all the *Mega Man* games. So even though he was not involved in some of them, I do believe that they are games produced under his methods, even if not by him.

Kitamura took the lion's share of inspiration for *Mega Man* from Japanese ranger shows like *Kamen Rider*, *Ninja Captor*, or the Super Sentai series, which was later rebranded for American audiences as *Mighty Morphin Power Rangers*. In a 2011 interview with artist Hitoshi Ariga for a Mega Man manga collection translated by fan website Shmuplations, Kitamura revealed that he wanted to replicate the story structures from those shows in what would eventually become *Mega Man*. The protagonists of *Super Sentai* or *Ninja Captor* are usually single-colored ranger heroes who do battle with a hokey, mostly off-stage villain who dispatches a new foe each week. American kids who came of age in the 90s might remember Rita Repulsa from *Power Rangers* sending a new monster after the titular teens each episode. Dr. Wily was originally conceived as a Rita Repulsa-esque villain, and the various Robot Masters were supposed to represent whatever monsters-of-the-week he'd ordered to kill the protagonist.

Mega Man too was born from this influence. Originally, Kitamura envisioned a white-colored protagonist similar to the legendary white rangers of many Japanese hero shows. The first character that Kitamura and fellow coders Nobuyuki Matsushima and Naoya Tomita designed was Cut Man, one of the original *Mega Man*'s Robot Masters, though he was originally intended to be the protagonist. Cut Man is instantly recognizable because of the giant scissors atop his head, an early design concept Kitamura hinged much of the gameplay on. Kitamura told Ariga, "In the beginning, I imagined a character like Mega Man equipped with some kind of weapon, but when you transformed, your whole appearance would change. You know that little protrusion on the top-front of Mega Man's helmet? When you changed weapons, it was supposed to change like the *Ninja Captor* characters' helmets, and show a little symbol depending on the weapon's element (fire, water, lightning, etc)." This, however, was ultimately scrapped when Nobuyuki Matsushima realized how much more compelling it would be to simply swap color palettes to represent the protagonist using a new weapon. Kitamura said, "It was a fresh, stylish idea, and this was when I started to get really excited about Mega Man's character design. This was also the point at which we decided to use the two sprites and two palettes for Mega Man's sprite. I was very grateful to Matsushima." The team used Cut Man as one of the monster-of-the-week villains and designed a protagonist inspired by a character from the *Time Bokan* anime, Tanpei—a genius boy sporting a blue jumpsuit and helmet equipped with cupcake-shaped cones. Despite the general silliness of this image, Kitamura sensed true sadness at Mega Man's core:

> Just the image of Mega Man standing [...] there's a sadness to it. Even his sprite has a certain gravity and seriousness to it [...]. When I see a young child playing alone, in a park or in the middle of the street, playing by himself [...] there's something so sad about that sight, it can almost bring me to tears. And there's something similarly lonely about Mega Man [...]. In the backstory I wrote, Mega Man alone is equipped with the functionality to turn himself off. That very fact imbues him with a sadness. The other robot masters were made for some kind of specific job or work, so there's no need for them to have an "off switch" they can control. However, a robot helper like Mega Man can make his own judgments, and therefore can decide whether he's needed or not [...]. The sadness of being a robot is having this inorganic existence.

As development wore on, the six members of the *Mega Man* team wrestled with the limits of the even-then-outdated Famicom hardware, a machine comprised of cheap, consumer-grade parts including a practically ancient 6502 microprocessor—the very same used in my parents' Atari 2600 released all the way back in 1977. While Kitamura and Inafune worked on designs for what would become the remaining Robot Masters, Manami Matsumae, a 23-year-old composer from Tokyo, wrote most of the soundtrack. Matsumae was fresh off composing for a mahjong video game, and although she'd go on to score some of Capcom's most famous titles—*Mercs*, *U.N. Squadron*, and *Magic Sword*—she remains best known for her work on the original *Mega Man*, a fast-paced soundtrack that's still covered and sampled by bands, hip hop artists, and DJs to this day. Matsumae was heavily influenced by Western rock music, and the Elec Man theme is actually a beat-for-beat reconstruction of Journey's "Faithfully." Look it up on YouTube. It's the exact same song.

Despite having respect for the quality of Matsumae's music on *Mega Man*, Kitamura didn't share her musical sensibilities. In a 2016 interview with Jeremy Parish, Matsumae explained that she wanted to channel "a near-futuristic space-oriented comic book, or manga" like *Astro Boy*, and "to make music that would go well with that kind of rhythm, match the movement of the game, how energetic it was." What Kitamura heard, however, was not that. For him, Matsumae was composing songs that tried to emulate the fundamental qualities of the Robot Masters: "On Elec Man's stage, she used these sounds that subtly suggest electricity. On Cut Man's stage, the music somehow gives me an impression of metal." Unsurprisingly, over the scant two months that Matsumae had to compose the sound effects and soundtrack, she "had to revise the music at times, to match what [Kitamura] was thinking." Kitamura wanted the rhythm to mimic the patterns of the player and enemies: If it was a fast-paced shooting level, the music should be fast-paced; if it was a more methodical puzzler, the music should be slow and contemplative. However, Kitamura and Matsumae never clicked artistically, and Kitamura had lingering doubts about the music even after the game's release.

To understand the importance of the music to the Mega Man team, it's helpful to remember Mega Man's original name. In Japan, they call him Rockman. This makes sense when we recall his supporting cast—his robot sister Roll (inspired by the popular Candy from the adorable manga *Candy Candy*) and later characters Blues, Bass, Tango, Beat, and Treble. To further differentiate *Rockman*—or the first *Mega Man* in the US—from its 2D competitors, Capcom wanted the game to focus on a soundtrack that was exponentially more complex than Koji Kondo's *Super Mario Bros.* score released just two years prior. If you discount power-up themes, level end melodies, and death dirges, the *Super Mario Bros.* soundtrack is comprised of only four unique tracks—themes for the overworld, underworld, water worlds, and castles. Each is extremely catchy but loops fairly quickly. The first *Rockman*, on the other hand, features eight unique stage tracks that are significantly longer than anything in *Super Mario Bros.*

Capcom of America—located in a concrete fortress in sunny Silicon Valley—didn't understand the game's seemingly strange fascination with rock music and, during the localization process, converted Rockman to Mega Man, a moniker that has stuck in the States to this day. When asked by *Game Players* in 1993 why the name was changed, former Capcom Vice President Joseph Morici bluntly replied, "The title was horrible."

Rockman wasn't the only name changed for the final product. From the earliest days of Atari and *Pong*, most game companies—with notable exceptions like Electronic Arts and Activision—went out of their way to keep individual developers out of the limelight, going so far as to require pseudonyms during end credits—if there were any end credits at all. In America, this was often an attempt to make a brand feel cohesive even if the development teams on various games rarely interacted. In Japan, this was to avoid poaching, a rampant practice in the 80s where rival game companies attempted to outbid employers for their best and brightest talent. Capcom used pseudonyms in all of their games, so Akira Kitamura, Keiji Inafune, Nobuyuki Matsushima, Naoya

Tomita, and Manami Matsumae became A.K., Inafking, H.M.D, TOM-PON, and Chanchacorin Manami in the game's credits across all regions. The *Mega Man* dev team bowed to the wishes of their corporate overlords, but the game industry was rapidly changing, and not everyone was happy with this arrangement. A fissure was widening in Capcom between those who believed game designers deserved their fair share of the credit and those who thought it should all go to Capcom, the almighty multinational brand.

Mega Man was released in 1987 to mediocre sales in both the Japanese and American markets. Inafune blamed the notoriously bad American box art for the game's numbers in the West—here, Mega Man is portrayed as a yellow/blue imp waving a revolver in front of what can only be described as a cyber-beachside clusterfuck—but that doesn't account for the game's reception in Japan. *Rockman*'s box art features the anime-inspired Mega Man we know and love today. Regardless, the *Rockman* project officially ended with no plans for a sequel, and Kitamura and Inafune were shuttled off to their next project, one Capcom was sure would outsell the underperforming *Rockman*—a game called *Pro Yakyuu? Satsujin Jiken!*, or *Professional Baseball? Murder Case!*

•

After pressing start, you're presented with *Mega Man 3*'s familiar stage select screen. Unlike the early Mario games or most NES platformers, the core *Mega Man* series is nonlinear. The player is allowed to pick which of Wily's eight Robot Masters and their corresponding stages to tackle first. Discovering the correct order is half the battle, as each Robot Master has a weakness that can be exploited by using a weapon stolen from a previously defeated boss. If you rush into Snake Man's stage without Needle Man's power-up, it's harder to win. Beat Needle Man first, and you snag his weapon and Snake Man's weakness.

Like the title screen, *Mega Man 3*'s stage select menu significantly differs from *Mega Man 2*. In *Mega Man 2*'s select screen, the Robot Masters' eight faces are assembled around a level you don't have access to that simply reads "Dr. Wily." You know the end from the very beginning. In *Mega Man 3*, the Dr. Wily box is replaced with Mega Man's face, his mouth frozen in uneasy smirk. As you guide the cursor around the screen trying to decide where to begin, Mega Man's robotic eyes creepily follow. If you move the cursor to Spark Man in the top left corner, Mega Man stares at Spark Man. Switch to Magnet Man directly beneath Mega Man, and he looks down, seemingly off-screen and into your living room.

The narrative effect this has on the game is slight but intriguing. Is Mega Man the final boss? Are you the villain? In *Mega Man 3*, there is very little narrative justification for why the player must hunt down and kill colorful robots. All you get are a few vague paragraphs from the manual:

Calling Mega Man! Calling Mega Man! Come in please!

Mega Man, we need you! We're down to the wire on our peace-keeping project. We've got to get those last energy crystals or we can't finish it. Dr. Wily is here now, too…yes…he's finally found his sanity. He knows where the crystals are! They're in the mining worlds, but we can't get to 'em. The robots are running amok and they're destroying everything!

You've got to get there, Mega Man, and get those crystals! You'll have to face some pretty mean metal. Expect the worst! Is Rush there with you? Give him a bolt to chew on and tell him it's from us. What's that…we must be getting static… sounds like you said 'Woof!'

Mega Man, get to those mining worlds pronto!
Grab the crystals and stop whoever's in charge!
He's one lunatic guy!

This is Dr. Light. Over and out!

The exposition dump in the manual is nonsensical at best and incomprehensible at worst, especially considering that many rental chains discarded game manuals before stocking their shelves. But, like most NES games, *Mega Man 3* shuttles you past its formal narrative at light speed.

•

By 1990, 30% of American households owned an NES, and every kid in my working-class Catholic school was as obsessed as I was. That fall, our teacher-nuns asked every student to subscribe to a magazine for a fundraiser. I scanned the cheap-looking pages of the catalogue and was stunned to discover *Nintendo Power*—a magazine about the NES! I was almost six and eager to combine my two deepest passions: reading and gaming.

Most of my friends selected *Nintendo Power* as well, and, in January, we received our first issues. The cover depicted a crudely illustrated Mega Man against the 8-bit pixel art of Dr. Wily's Castle. Bright aqua letters beneath the masthead proclaimed *"MEGA MAN III: TEST YOUR METTLE ON A NEW 'MEGA' MISSION!"* Under the familiar Official Nintendo Seal of Quality sat a red and yellow banner proclaiming *Nintendo Power* as "*THE SOURCE FOR NEWS AND STRATEGIES STRAIGHT FROM THE PROS.*" I nearly choked on my after-school milk. This was the greatest thing I'd ever seen.

Volume 20 of *Nintendo Power* is 99 pages of nostalgic power pop. A full-page spread near the end highlights the reveal of the Super Famicom in Tokyo. A celebrity profile describes "Donnie Wahlburg"—his name is misspelled repeatedly throughout the New Kids on the Block fluff piece—as "a confirmed Nintendo maniac." The reader mail features a letter from Apple genius Steve Wozniak about earning a high score on *Tetris* while flying across continents. There's even a *Bart vs. the Space Mutants* poster I hung proudly in my bedroom until my late-twenties. *Nintendo Power* volume 20 is a time capsule, and nothing grabbed my attention more than the twenty-page strategy guide for *Mega Man 3* that ran immediately after the letters.

In retrospect, it's easy to see why I was so captivated by the *Mega Man 3* section. The game's place on the cover immediately makes it obvious it's the best game in the issue, and the other games that receive multipage spreads—*The Immortal, Déjà Vu,* and *Gremlins 2*—didn't appeal to me in the least. I found myself strangely moved by the image of Mega Man on page 8. Half his body is the hero child we recognize. The other is an x-ray scan of his insides, a jigsaw of steel and fiber-optics. Even then, I felt different from other children, a sinking feeling that my insides weren't exactly the same, that I wasn't human enough and never really could be. I probably seemed outgoing, but I was afraid I couldn't feel emotions as deeply as other people and was walled off from them somehow. Although I couldn't articulate it at age six, I weirdly related to Mega Man and what I misinterpreted as his Pinocchio-esque quest to become real, to fully feel like everyone else.

The next twenty pages feature detailed explanations of Mega Man's many collectible power-ups and maps of the game's levels. I sat in my grandfather's basement and traced my index finger across those beautiful pixelated maps, pretending that I was really playing, that I was actually navigating the Blue Bomber past mechanical foes and obstacles. Eventually, my parents agreed to rent the game, and I returned from Blockbuster on a Friday afternoon giddy and hyper, a weekend of neon-coated gaming ahead of me.

I spent the next 72 hours holed up in what my family referred to as the back room—adjacent to the larger living room and kitchen, home to a small loveseat, fish tank, and wooden console complete with CRTV and Nintendo—darting back and forth between the strategies in *Nintendo Power* and the robotic obstacles on my TV screen. It was the first time I'd experienced the marriage of text—*Nintendo Power*—and digital artifact—*Mega Man 3*—and I was captivated by the possibilities of two seemingly disparate mediums working in tandem. Even though I couldn't beat any of the initial Robot Masters save for Needle Man, I was utterly enthralled. Success didn't matter. Up until that point, I'd only managed to beat *Chip 'n Dale Rescue Rangers*—another Keiji Inafune game, unbeknownst to me at the time—and it was so rewarding to fail, fail, fail again, before making a tiny step forward into new and uncharted territory. By the time my parents returned to Blockbuster on Sunday afternoon, *Mega Man 3* was my favorite NES game I didn't own.

That should have made it a top priority on my Christmas list the following winter, but I never even asked for it. Ten months is an eternity for a child, and, by the following Christmas, I wanted two games more than anything else—*DuckTales* and the Sistine Chapel of 8-bit platformers, *Super Mario Bros. 3*. I didn't play *Mega Man 3* again, or any of the NES Mega Man games, for years, and soon Nintendo's incessant hype train had moved on to the greener, 16-bit pastures of the Super Nintendo.

For me, *Mega Man 3* became more than a sequel, more than a classic platformer released in the final blush of the NES's heyday. *Mega Man 3* and its spread in *Nintendo Power* symbolized the exact moment when I realized there was an entire adult world out there actively engaged in writing and thinking about video games. My realization that some adults took gaming as seriously as I did laid the groundwork for everything to come.

•

As far as first stage strategy goes, I always choose Needle Man. I can't definitively say it's easier than beginning with Top Man—the preferred choice of many of *Mega Man 3*'s speedrunners—but it's the only path that worked for me as a child, and it now feels destined and legendary, hardwired into my brain. Like most of the series's levels, Needle Man's stage is a futuristic mish-mash of candy-colored inconsistencies. You appear on solid yellow ground that might be an interconnected microchip or maybe shipping containers, and as you move through the stage, the landscape deteriorates into some kind of robot pirate ship. Why a boss named Needle Man—he's literally just a blue Kool-Aid Man with a handful of needles protruding from his head— would live in a robot pirate ship is beyond me, especially since the level was a golden opportunity to unleash Pirate Man, a character Capcom wouldn't unveil until 1998's Japanese-only *Rockman & Forte* for the Super Famicom.

Adding to the absurdity are the main enemies you encounter: a series of pink robot armadillos who either roll in a ball and crush you or shoot a semicircle of needles that covers a large swath of the screen. *Nintendo Power* inexplicably refers to these creatures as "Needle Harry." All of this nicely sets you up for the overwhelming surrealism of the *Mega Man* franchise. The *Mega Man 3* team isn't interested in designing a world that links together in a way that makes literal sense à la *Metal Gear*—an NES game with a semi-realistic military base as a game map—but is more concerned with stages that convey a dreamlike experience.

Once you advance beyond the initial Needle Harrys and descend into the robot pirate ship proper, you're faced with snaking tunnels defended by one row of falling spikes after another. You encounter similar obstacles in the Super Mario games or pretty much any NES-era platformer, and, in those, you simply run as fast as you can to escape. That would have been your only option in *Mega Man 2*, but if you try that here, Mega Man dies in a disturbing explosion of pulsing yellow light. There are no in-game hints, and unless you have the manual or a copy of *Nintendo Power*, you might flail wildly before discovering that if you press down and A simultaneously, Mega Man will slide. This opens up so many new strategies that I often feel like calling the debate between *Mega Man 2* and *3* right there. The slide! *MM3* has it. *MM2* doesn't. What else needs to be said? Regardless, once you discover the slide, Capcom demands that you master Mega Man's new technique immediately. Time the slides wrong and you careen feet-first into the needles and die.

Have I mentioned that Mega Man now has a pink robot dog named Rush? Because Mega Man now has a pink robot dog named Rush. If you were expecting some kind of cutscene explaining why Mega Man now has a mechanical mutt companion, you haven't been paying attention to how little *Mega Man 3* values narrative. Halfway through the Needle Man stage, you encounter a blue energy tank sitting precariously atop a floating platform just out of reach. Energy tanks, your Get Out of Jail Free cards in the Mega Man series, allow you to pause the game and immediately refill your health. Collecting as many of these as possible is vital to surviving some of the game's more difficult boss encounters, especially during the final stages. But the first one you encounter is literally impossible to nab using any of Mega Man's core abilities. And to make matters worse, there's a Needle Harry walled off at the bottom-right hand of the screen, and every few seconds he spits out a new batch of spikes.

Some energy tanks are only accessible after acquiring a specific weapon from a fallen Robot Master, so a novice player might give up on this particular trinket and try again later. However, if you gleaned anything from the spike room just a handful of screens earlier, you might wade into the pause screen and discover that if you scroll down far enough, Mega Man already has a selectable power up with the letters RC next to it. Choose it, and Mega Man reappears on the screen in a spiffy pink and white uniform—much like Kitamura's transforming ranger characters. Tap the B button, and Rush will magically descend from the sky, a coil extending from his little puppy back. Nothing explicitly tells you what to do, but even a child can sense it. Move a few steps away from the dog, rush forward, and leap onto the coil. Just as you expect, Mega Man flies into the air and lands on the platform with the energy tank. If you're a dog person like me, it doesn't matter that none of this makes sense. All that matters is that Capcom added the one thing to *Mega Man* that always makes everything better: a radical canine down for adventure.

After mastering the slide and Rush Coil, you reach the end of the level and the long-awaited bout with Needle Man. Like all of the Robot Masters, Needle Man is a finely tuned mix of patterns and simulated randomness. The boss encounters in Mega Man games all take place in a one-screen room no bigger than the playfields in early arcade games like *Donkey Kong* or *Space Invaders*. It's basically Thunderdome: Two robots enter, one robot leaves. If you inch too close to Needle Man, he'll bend over and stab you with the needle on his head. If you stay on the opposite side of the screen, he'll leap up and down and shoot a seemingly random spread of spikes. When he jumps in your direction, slide out of the way—see again how Capcom already expects you to master the new mechanics or face death—and continue shooting ad nauseum until Needle Man explodes.

A commonly held belief among developers is that the opening level of a well-programmed game teaches the player what thematic rules to anticipate going forward. By the end of the Needle Man stage, you've collected three essential supplies. First, you get Needle Man's weapon, the Needle Cannon, which is selectable at any time and has its own ammo supply just like every other weapon you obtain from a Robot Master. The second item is one of the reasons why I always go after Needle Man first. The Rush Jet is a power-up for your dog that turns him into a flying skateboard allowing you to sail past the game's most difficult jumping sections. The final prize isn't for Mega Man, but for you, the player: a password, your only true lifeline in a game that thrives on brutality. By this point, you've also mastered the slide and Rush Coil and discovered your first energy tank. The first level of *Mega Man 3* teaches you that you're incomplete without your trinkets, that you're an empty husk at the game's outset. You must collect more and more and more.

•

I rekindled my NES obsession in 1999. I'd just started high school and had long ago traded in my NES and small handful of games for the Super Nintendo, then a PlayStation and the epic, cutscene-heavy *Final Fantasy VII*. After much pleading, my family finally purchased a desktop computer, and, on one fine day, my pal Mike came over after school and showed me Nesticle.

Nesticle is credited as the first significant MS-DOS emulator of NES games, but what I really loved about it as a fourteen-year-old professional goober was its name. Designed by a hacker named Sardu at the over-the-top Bloodlust Software, an emulator named "Nesticle" is the kind of crude joke that truly speaks to an angsty teenage boy, the pun equivalent of doodling decapitated Donald Ducks in a geometry notebook. Double-click Nesticle, and you're treated to a bare-bones menu, your cursor transformed into a severed hand hemorrhaging gallons of cartoony blood. In the hidden corners of the internet, Mike and I tracked down ROM after

ROM of downloadable NES games and soon were playing *Mega Man 3* for hours at a time. Although the experience wasn't exactly the same—using a keyboard could never sniff the simplicity of the NES controller, and there was always something off about seeing the flickering sprites of your childhood blown up boxy and clear on a computer monitor—that afternoon reignited something I assumed I'd outgrown.

There's an instant gratification to NES games that video games as a whole had begun to move away from as far back as 1999. I'd recently been obsessed with story-heavy epics like the 60-hour plus *Xenogears* and the long-winded, often insane *Metal Gear Solid*. For the most part, NES games avoid complex narrative, and what's left is a simple imperative of fun above all else. *Mega Man 3* has no time for a well-developed story. You run, jump, shoot, die, and repeat until your fingers are blistered.

For the next five years, I still obsessively played every major release for the PlayStation and then the PlayStation 2, but I always returned to Nesticle and the seemingly infinite possibilities of the NES library, everything from fondly recalled games of my youth like *Dragon Warrior* to forgotten platforming miracles like *Little Samson*. And always I wondered, what happened to my physical NES, and should I find another? During the summer between my freshman and sophomore years of college, I was cleaning out my parents' basement and discovered a few of my original NES games: *Super Mario Bros.*, *DuckTales*, *Rescue Rangers*. In a strange confluence of events, my friend Jack told me he'd found his NES in his basement and was willing to sell it for five dollars since he couldn't get it to work. I happily handed him a wrinkled Lincoln earned from long hours selling iPods at Target, and for the first time in thirteen years hooked an NES to my parents' television.

The screen blinked alive, but no game would play.

In the 80s, if you couldn't get a Nintendo game to start, you were left with two options: you could either plug the game into a Game Genie and hope that connection worked better, or you could literally blow into the game. In 2004, I logged on to the few web forums still dedicated to 8-bit games and discovered that the infamous NES screen flashes were caused by faulty connections between the green PCB board at the base of every NES cartridge and the 72-pin connector inside the NES's opening. Following detailed instructions online, I cleaned my NES cartridges with a Q-tip soaked in Windex. Then I used a screwdriver to pry open my NES—its internal galaxies at last revealed to me as a dusty green motherboard—and removed the 72-pin connector, an electronic set of teeth. These slow and methodical rituals were strangely soothing. As a college freshman, I was just beginning to wrestle with anxiety, and what calmed me even more than returning to the colorful worlds of my childhood were the repeated gestures of swabbing a PCB board clean and examining it beneath a lamp to make sure it was dry. Once the 72-pin connector was removed, I called the Nintendo hotline—their hold music was a poppy remix of the familiar overworld theme from *Super Mario Bros.*—and requested a replacement. Even in 2004, Nintendo still supported a system released two decades earlier.

The new 72-pin connector arrived a few days later, and, after a quick installation, Jack's NES was finally working. I could at last return to the Mushroom Kingdom the way it was intended to be experienced— on a shitty TV with an NES controller. It was a magical moment, one in which even my parents—long lapsed from their *Lost Luggage* days—sat down to laugh and play and reminisce. That should have been the end of the story, a momentary return to childhood before I marched into adulthood proper. But then, a few days later, while accompanying Jack and Mike to check out the latest PlayStation 2 games at Funcoland, I spotted a stack of discounted NES games on a table. I ran my fingers across the labels—so smooth, so reassuring!— and came across *Fester's Quest*, a game I owned as a child but hadn't found in my basement. It was only 99 cents! Wouldn't it be cool to track down the four or five other games I'd owned as a kid? Wasn't *Fester's Quest* worth the price of a candy bar?

A few weeks later, I drove to Pittsburgh to visit my college girlfriend and dragged her all across western Pennsylvania hunting down NES cartridges. I returned home with a sack of games from Goodwill. When I showed my father, he said he didn't remember us owning *Maniac Mansion* or *Teenage Mutant Ninja Turtles II: The Arcade Game*. That's because we hadn't, but they were only a few dollars each! How could I pass up such amazing deals?

I spent the first night of sophomore year playing *Track and Field II* on the Power Pad—a barely functioning mat you physically jog on to make your avatar move—and a dozen other NES games I kept in a Rubbermaid beneath my twin bed. I drove to a flea market where I convinced empty-nest mothers to sell me *Punch-Out!!* at a discount, a pawnshop where I slid dollar bills to tellers behind bulletproof glass for a label-damaged copy of *Arkanoid*, a game store where I negotiated prices on *Metroid* and *Goonies II*, a record shop where I discovered six of Wisdom Tree's seven Bible-themed NES games beneath a stack of VHS tapes for just two dollars a pop. I printed out a checklist of every single NES game complete with rarity levels for each game. I owned ten games, then twenty, then fifty, then seventy, each of them cleaned carefully with a

Q-tip. When friends asked why I kept buying beyond my original childhood collection, why I blew money on Bible games that weren't even fun, I told them I was going to own them all. I was going to find every last Nintendo game.

Like Mega Man, I too would finally become complete.

•

If the spatial absurdity of Needle Man's stage exists in stark contrast to the cleanly laid-out geography of *Metal Gear* or *Castlevania*, the Snake Man level pushes that insanity even further. Most of the stage exists atop and inside a giant, mechanical snake outfitted with a dozen heads that puke fire. What lives inside this horrifying creature, you ask? Pole vaulting robots who go ignored by *Nintendo Power* but are retroactively labeled Bubukan by The Mega Man Knowledge Base, a dense Wikipedia of Blue Bomber esoterica. The MMKB claims that the Bubukan—basically Slinkys with googly eyes who vault forward on plungers—were built by Dr. Light for something called the Robot Olympics. The MMKB even reports that the Bubukan were inspired by Ukrainian pole vaulter Sergey Bubka, but it's unclear whether that was a clever act of anarchy on the part of the American localization team or someone from Capcom in Japan.

There's something off-putting about the Bubukan, some fleeting sensation that you're witnessing a joke riffing on cultural touchstones you don't have access to. Unfortunately for Capcom, this wasn't the first time their attempts at parody were met with crickets by an unaffected market.

•

Famicom games don't resemble their American counterparts. The gray Game Paks American thirty-somethings grew up on are bulky and serious, spiritual successors to the VHS just as the NES replicated the VCR. Famicom games are squat and half the length of American NES games, more like cassettes for the ultra-successful Sony Walkman. They come in a variety of colors, everything from lime green to hot pink. Keiji Inafune's *Pro Yakyuu? Satsujin Jiken!* or *Professional Baseball? Murder Case!* is decked out in fetching aqua, and, like every other Famicom game, you can't just insert it into an American NES and expect it to work. Famicom PCB boards have 60 pins at the bottom while NES games have 72. Famicom games won't fit inside the NES's pin connector. Technologically, the games are basically the same, but this small difference made it difficult for American players to import Japanese games before they hit US shores. A few fly-by-night companies produced adapters, but your only other option for playing Japanese games was to import a Famicom or famiclone—a cheap, knockoff version, many of which sold incredibly well in China, Russia, and Japan.

I foolishly chose a famiclone for my initial *Professional Baseball? Murder Case!* excursion. I'm no stranger to importing, and I'm intimately familiar with the shoddy copyediting on black market boxes, but my famiclone, the amazingly named Play Computer Dash, should have given me an idea of how things would end. The machine itself is cast in the familiar red and white of the Famicom, but it looks more like a waffle iron with a slot in the center. The tagline, prominent on the box, reads: "*THIS IS COMPATABILITY MACHINE. LET'S PLAY GAME. EVERYBODY GETS FUN.*" Nothing could be further from the truth.

I plugged the Chinese AC adapter into my surge protector, and within seconds of firing up the Play Computer Dash, it was popping and smoking, the signal on my television a curious blink. Perhaps this was an omen of the game to come.

Professional Baseball? Murder Case! begins with an unnecessary disclaimer reminding the player that this is a work of fiction. Although dedicated fans have trans-lated ROMs of Japanese 8-bit, text-heavy classics like *Final Fantasy II* or *Portopia*, no translation of *Professional Baseball? Murder Case!* currently exists. Luckily, Boss

Fight Books Associate Editor Michael P. Williams provided a translation to aid my fumbling exploits through Capcom's baseball parody. Our protagonist is Suguru Igawa, a sports analyst and former pitcher of the fictional Ganants baseball club. While watching TV from the comfort of his home, Igawa sees a news report announcing the murder of Nobuyasu Harada, a Tokyo Printing Company employee found slain in the Princess Hotel parking garage. There's a knock on Igawa's door, and we're introduced to the weeping Tatsunori Hora, a Ganant teammate, who tells Igawa he happened to be in the parking garage at the time of the murder and might have been set up by a rival pitcher and rogue reporter. Suddenly, the police burst in, and despite Igawa's protests, they name both Hora and Igawa as suspects. Hora flees, and Igawa is left to his own devices to clear his name by finding the true murderer.

Professional Baseball? Murder Case! resembles *Dragon Warrior* or *Final Fantasy* more than the original *Mega Man*. You find yourself in a top-down view of contemporary Tokyo. Many credit *Mother*, the predecessor to the Super Nintendo's *EarthBound*, as the first RPG set in the present, but *Professional Baseball? Murder Case!* beat it to market by seven months. Your goal is to slowly unravel the murder of Nobuyasu Harada by collecting clues all over Japan by foot, car, train, and ferry. Unfortunately, every step decreases your Life Points, and the overworld map is patrolled by bands of police. Encounter an officer and you may be able to smooth talk your way out of a fight, but otherwise, you're shuttled not to a JRPG-style battle where two groups stand sentry politely waiting for the other to attack. Instead, you enter an *Ikari Warriors*-esque top-down shooter where you hurl baseballs at raging cops. It's a bizarre battle system for a game truly ahead of its time. Over the course of your adventure, Igawa will dress in drag, hang out in gay bars, pal around with ghosts, meet the actual President of Capcom, and unravel a plot involving sports corruption, counterfeit cash, and murder. The game is clearly a parody of Namco's *Pro Yakyuu* baseball games, a long-running and much-celebrated series in Japan, and *Professional Baseball? Murder Case!* even ends with a *Pro Yakyuu*-styled minigame where Igawa must compete for the pennant. Squint hard enough and you may notice that the umpire looks suspiciously like Mega Man, the character Kitamura and Inafune actually wanted to work on.

After the so-so sales of the first Mega Man installment, Capcom hesitated on funding a sequel. Instead, Kitamura and Inafune were moved on to *Professional Baseball? Murder Case!* under the belief that this quirky baseball parody would be more financially successful than *Rockman*. Kitamura and Inafune, however, were skeptical, and, after a great deal of protesting, convinced Capcom to fund development for a sequel on two conditions: (1) They had to finish *Professional Baseball?* *Murder Case!* first; (2) They had to program *Mega Man 2* on their own time. This meant that the sequel was mostly coded at night, after a full day of working on Capcom's baseball parody. *Professional Baseball? Murder Case!* was eventually released in Japan to a lackluster response on Christmas Eve 1988, and now it's mostly remembered for being released the same day as *Rockman 2*, a game that would alter Capcom and the Famicom forever.

•

After vaulting across a series of chimneys, you reach your star-crossed confrontation with Snake Man. One of the biggest criticisms of the Mega Man series as a whole is that a large swath of bosses is rendered completely impotent if you have the correct weapon to defeat them. Snake Man is one of the chief offenders. His room is littered with peaks and valleys, and if you get stuck in one of the shallow holes, Snake Man will relentlessly fire at you from above. His attack is the strangest in a game full of bizarre moments. Snake Man shoots mechanical snakes out of his arm that slither across the ground and bite you. Equip the Needle Cannon from the previous level, and you only have to hit Snake Man a handful of times before he explodes. His death, like all of the Robot Masters, is still a satisfying preview of the mayhem yet to come.

11

IF YOU BELIEVED THAT SNAKE MAN'S quick defeat indicated an easy journey ahead, the Gemini Man level smashes those illusions to dust. This relentless stage is typically where I stop if I'm casually playing on a lazy, basketball-less Sunday. And even though it usually results in me slamming my fist into my couch, the level's difficulty grows more and more refreshing with each year and console generation. NES games usually had to be difficult because otherwise they'd be too short. Look up any retro speedrunners online. These are the best players on earth, and they can usually handle difficult games like *Mega Man*, *Contra*, or *Metal Gear* in just a few minutes. That's because NES games are comprised of tiny amounts of data. 1993's *Kirby's Adventure* is one of the largest NES games at only six megabytes. For comparison's sake, a modern PC game can easily eclipse 10,000 megabytes. 8-bit developers had to pad out length with difficulty, but modern developers don't. Because of this, there's something unexpected about returning to NES games and experiencing true challenge. So many modern games feel like beautiful treadmills—take, for example, *Final Fantasy XIII* or *BioShock*—where the player is guaranteed a win as long as they log enough hours. *Mega Man 3* and its ilk provide no guarantees. Memorizing and mastering its traps and boss patterns might take weeks, months, or, in my case, decades. Meanwhile, I completed *Grand Theft Auto V* in just a few weeks. There's a sharpened purity to *Mega Man 3* I still crave after all these years, a sensation of true struggle and achievement that's often difficult to find in modern gaming.

At the start of Gemini Man's stage, Mega Man beams down onto what appears to be an icy moon blanketed by darkness. Early on, you approach a hole in the ice plugged up by a glowing cork. The game freezes, and for the first time you hear a mournful yet instantly recognizable whistle. It calls back to the opening theme, and out of the sky appears another robot who looks suspiciously like Mega Man himself. Red instead of blue, this new character carries a shield, his cape blowing in the wind, a nod to Mega Man's swaying hair in the opening of *Mega Man 2*. We know him today as Proto Man, the antihero rival of the NES Mega Man games, but he was referred to as Break Man near the end of *Mega Man 3* and in *Nintendo Power*. This was meant to save the twist that he's a prototype for the end of the game, but since that revelation is handled pretty clumsily—not to mention that the Break Man moniker is only used once in the game and barely remembered at all today—I'll refer to him as Proto Man from here on out.

Proto Man, called Blues in Japan despite wearing almost entirely red, is another reason why some of us prefer *Mega Man 3* to its predecessor. Mega Man is noble and courageous and mostly a stand-in for the player à la Super Mario, but Proto Man's allegiances and intentions are unclear to the player and even to himself. While some Robot Masters like Snake Man and Needle Man look like they're part of the same extended family as Mega Man, Proto Man is nearly a reskin of the titular character. "We wanted people to be unsure whether Proto Man was a friend or a foe. On the one hand, he'd seem like a rival to Mega Man, but at the same time he'd seem like a comrade," Keiji Inafune wrote in 2008's *Mega Man: Official Complete Works*—a 20th anniversary art book. A common trope in Japanese ranger series is to introduce a shadowy mystery character who occasionally helps the protagonist or stands in their way midway-through the story. It's unclear whose side the character is on, and often this new rogue is a long-lost brother of the central hero. Akira Kitamura said to Hitoshi Ariga that in *Mega Man 3* he hoped to "Introduce a new prototype robot, No. 000 (he would be Mega Man's mysterious brother)," and took his inspiration from the popular show *Kikaider*, whose main character is a half-blue, half-red cyborg with a human alter ego. Interestingly, whenever Kikaider's human counterpart announces the cyborg's arrival, he plays a repetitive trumpet melody similar to Proto Man's whistle. In the haphazard lore of the Mega Man series, Proto Man is— as his English name suggests—Dr. Light's first attempt at an independent cyborg in the style of Mega Man. Unfortunately, his power core is defective, and fearing that Dr. Light's repairs might alter his personality, Proto Man chooses to wander the earth until his energy finally runs out. Later, he's discovered by Dr. Wily, who fixes him without altering Proto Man's personality. All Wily asks is that Proto Man helps him defeat Mega Man. This, even though it's never directly addressed in the game or manual, sets the events of *Mega Man 3* into motion.

If Mega Man is the squeaky clean Andy Hardy of the futuristic robot world, Proto Man is James Dean, nothing but cocksure charisma and attitude. In the official art book, the pencil rendering for Mega Man in *Mega Man 3* has the titular character awkwardly bending one knee and gesturing wildly with his arms, his pained frown the telltale sign of a man holding in a fart. Proto Man, in his stylish red and gray armor, leans confidently against his shield, his radical sunglasses reflecting twin beams of light, his yellow scarf dancing in the wind. Mega Man is a character for children, Proto Man is for their older siblings experimenting with cigarettes and sex and booze. Their rivalry—in which Proto Man repeatedly interrupts your progress through the game either to fight or help you—is the most daring addition to the game and the play mechanic that separates *Mega Man 3* from the first two entries in the series.

For Proto Man's introduction, Capcom once again chooses to avoid a text-heavy break in the action. Later Mega Man installments on the PlayStation would bog down the gameplay with long-winded anime cutscenes that never amounted to anything more than explaining which robots were bad. Kitamura told Ariga that, "In an action game, I don't think the story should interrupt the action." *Mega Man 3* has no time for excess. Mega Man discovers a giant cork blocking his path. The mysterious character Proto Man appears. The two stare at each other, noting the uncanny resemblance. Then Proto Man blows up the cork and teleports away. That's narrative distilled to its most essential, childlike form, and the player knows as sure as they know anything that they will encounter this character again.

If *Mega Man 3* was produced today as a blockbuster, mega-studio release in the vein of *Uncharted* or *Far Cry*, you better believe that the introduction of Proto Man would not be handled in the retro minimalist manner of 1990. Instead, all semblance of control would be wrestled away from the player and a tedious cutscene would ensue. Take, for example, *DuckTales Remastered*, the high definition 2013 re-release of another Capcom NES classic. (Keiji Inafune was coincidentally a sprite designer on the original.) *DuckTales Remastered* debuted on Xbox 360, PlayStation 3, Wii U, and PC, and despite using the same level layouts as its NES predecessor, the game resembles the Disney cartoon more than its blocky 8-bit cousin. What was once a quirky platforming romp with little to no narrative is fattened up for the remake. Nearly every time Scrooge enters a new screen, the player loses control and a drawn-out cutscene explains a narrative that when boiled down mimics 50 Cent's mantra—"get rich or die trying." *DuckTales Remastered* is an outright mockery of everything that made NES games like *Mega Man 3* and the original *DuckTales* great: an imperative of player-controlled gameplay over developer-controlled narrative. As the cutscene-heavy aesthetic of so many major developers is slowly falling out of vogue and more games return to the player-directed narratives of the 1980s, *Mega Man 3* and its 8-bit ilk serve as not only a reminder of where video games began, but also where they might still go.

•

Before I began college in 2003, I spent most of my time online chatting with randos on Instant Messenger or slowly downloading albums from Napster. By the time I graduated in 2007, my co-ed brethren and I were already entrenched in what we now recognize as the modern web. We uploaded photos to Facebook and watched YouTube nearly as much —if not more than—TV. Scroll back far enough in my external hard drive of collegiate photos— most of which are so booze-soaked that all traces have been deleted from the internet—and you'll find a 2006 picture of me on my enormous and comically un-portable laptop watching *The Angry Video Game Nerd*. Even then, I recognized that *AVGN*'s appearance on my computer screen signaled a sea change, that soon my weird little hobby that endeared me to nerds would march bravely into the sterilizing light of the mainstream. I knew this moment was so important that I literally had a photo taken for posterity.

Born in Haddonfield, New Jersey, in 1980, the Angry Video Game Nerd—birth name James Rolfe— grew up obsessed with filmmaking, monster movies, and video games. While attending the University of the Arts of Philadelphia, Rolfe produced a number of student films under the banner of his Cinemassacre production company. Rolfe told me that, "Making movies for me wasn't really about making movies, it was making art [...] finding the best way to express myself." Rolfe's student films are short and nonsensical, plots and allegiances shift rapidly, and everything feels a tad ADD—the films range from horror to animation to comedy to music videos and back again—as if Rolfe's breakneck sensibilities required a medium more constrained than film.

He discovered the perfect vehicle for his talents in 2004. While living with his parents after graduation, Rolfe filmed two short segments for a VHS series he produced that collected his best work. The final two clips on *The Cinemassacre Gold Collection* VHS are "Bad NES Games: Simon's Quest" and "Bad NES Games: Jekyll and Hyde." Both videos are less than ten minutes long and feature Rolfe as a raging nerd reviewing terrible Nintendo games released two decades prior. Many of the staples of the Angry Video Game Nerd persona are present even in this analog format, two years before Rolfe's series hit YouTube. The Angry Video Game Nerd—though he's unnamed here—is a foul-mouthed Nintendo fanboy complete with white collar shirt and pocket protector. In character, Rolfe throws back Yuengling after Yuengling and shouts things like:

> Never play it because you will be wishing for the rest of your life that you can invent a time machine and go back to the day you played that game and just fucking kill yourself […]. If you

ever find this game [...] smash it with a hammer. Smash it till every tiny fragment is like so small it's invisible [...]. You'd rather superglue your asshole shut than play that game. You'd rather drown yourself in gasoline.

This kind of crude, over-the-top analysis quickly became the calling card for the entire series. The gag, as described by Rolfe in the "What Was I Thinking?: The Making of *The Angry Video Game Nerd*" featurette from his Volume 1 DVD, is deceptively simple. "Why would anyone bother to complain about a game that's so old, and why would they still be playing it? That's the whole joke."

It wasn't until 2006 that friend and long-term collaborator Mike Matei convinced Rolfe to continue the series. This time, however, Rolfe ditched VHS in favor of YouTube. The reaction was almost instantaneous. The most popular *Angry Video Game Nerd* videos have been viewed between five million and ten million times, and his work was covered in mainstream venues like MTV as far back as 2006. A year after his YouTube debut, GameTrailers signed a contract with Rolfe to produce two episodes per month, allowing him to quit his day job and focus on *AVGN* full-time. The gig culminated in both a full-length feature film and a video game for PlayStation 3, Xbox 360, 3DS, and PC.

The genius of James Rolfe is that he figured out before anyone else how to tap into Millennial and Gen X gamer nostalgia in a mainstream way. *AVGN* is not just one ornery nerd in his parents' basement who'd rather spend hours dissecting the minutia behind *Mega Man 3* over the latest first-person shooter crapped out by Microsoft subsidiaries. The widespread success of *The Angry Video Game Nerd* was an SOS call across the internet that announced to retro gamers around the world that they were not alone. I was comforted by *AVGN* and his legion of fans posting support in the comments. We were all right, and everything was OK. I wasn't alone, nor was it strange to obsessively collect hunks of plastic discarded in childhood. I had proof right on my computer screen. While playing *Super Mario Bros.*, or *Dragon Warrior*, or *Mega Man 3*, I could, if only briefly, shut out all fears of global warming, the looming recession, and my overdrawn bank account. As Rolfe told me himself, "Retro games are current now […] before nobody was interested in those games, and now everyone is. Now everyone's taken it into the current generation […] It doesn't matter if it's old or new. It's moved on to something bigger."

•

After Proto Man clears your path, you drop into the ice moon, the center of which is a Cronenberg-esque biological prison. The tunnels here are constructed of neon orbs of organic matter, and in the first stretch of this new subterranean world, your only obstacles are Fish Eggs arranged in dense patterns that stretch from floor to ceiling blocking your path. Is it ethical for Mega Man to open fire on a colony of unborn fish? Capcom never asks you to wrestle with this question. The world of Mega Man is bound by one rule: forward! All progress is justifiable, even if said justice requires a robot child to mow down Fish Egg after Fish Egg inside the organic husk of an ice moon. Furiously tap the B button and discover that with each Fish Egg you destroy, a new Torpedo Fish spawns. These robot babies fly at you— the main attack of most Mega Man villains—and yet again you're left with no option but to incinerate them. This all sounds gruesome—especially once you discover that if you shoot the eggs in the correct order you can build stairs to power-ups otherwise out of reach—but in *Mega Man 3*, the happy-go-lucky charm almost never falters, the upbeat chip music never stops.

The penultimate section of the Gemini Man stage is by far the most difficult expanse we've encountered so far. A loose collection of organic blocks extends from the start of the area to the end, and if you fall into the murky waters below, you will die. Making matters worse are the Dragon Flies that dive-bomb you from above and the robot fish below who shoot torpedoes at you from their backs. Along the way are barely submerged platforms atop which sit an extra life and an all-important energy tank. Here, you're presented with a true existential dilemma. Do you: (a) leap into the otherwise deadly waters, nab the collectible, and use the Rush Coil to spring back to the path; or (b) continue on as before and acknowledge you don't have the ability or skill to track down every last collectible? I can't advise you, but I will say that here I died again and again and again, my controller slippery with sweat.

This stretch is the reason why I never beat *Mega Man 3* as a kid. I'd reach a section like this and die, die, die. I'd continue and die, die, die again and eventually quit. It requires focus and resolve, and in a game like *Mega Man 3* where you can at any time switch to another level, I didn't have the patience I did in a game like *Contra*, where there is only one predetermined path forward. If you're stuck on the ice level in *Contra*, you can't switch to the fortress instead. The level-selecting freedom of *Mega Man 3* actually had the opposite effect on me as a kid. I saw more of the game than I did in something linear and unspeakably difficult like *Dragon's Lair*, but I only experienced the openings of each introductory level. As an adult, I have the patience to persist—not to mention a Nintendo 3DS port of the game that allows you to save anywhere—even though my reflexes are dulled and my hands claw up after an hour like an arthritic grandfather.

If you're able to survive this section, you're rewarded with a bout with Gemini Man, the most difficult Robot Master you've fought so far. Even while using the Search Snake, the fight is brutal. The battle begins when Gemini Man immediately clones himself. Then he leaps to the left and runs across the length of the stage back to the right. His doppelgänger does the same. You'll be able to win once you understand the pattern, but this will take a few tries if you're not using a guide. And unless you arrived with a war chest of lives, expect to replay the entire level—complete with the difficult jumping section—at least once. But when you do crack the pattern, you're once again confronted with the surreal dissonance of Capcom's quirky platformer. This isn't Mario yanking a lever to drop a monster into a pit of lava. That at least makes some kind of procedural sense. Here, you fire tiny miniature snakes that chomp along an organic ice floor until they explode on impact into Gemini Man's clone. Land enough tiny robot snakes, and he dies. Your reward is the eponymous Gemini Laser, taking you one step closer to completing your collection of mechanical trinkets.

•

In 2007, just a few months after stumbling across *Angry Video Game Nerd*, I finished college and moved to Pittsburgh for graduate school. Like many grads, I was stunned to discover that adult life—or at least the funhouse version provided by grad school—was depressingly lonely. I was no longer surrounded by people at all hours of the day, and I rarely, if ever, met friends my own age. Most of my peers were five, ten, sometimes twenty years older, and although we got along well, they had obligations that prevented them from drinking all night and playing *Contra* until three a.m. I wasted so many weekends that first semester in Pittsburgh guzzling Yuengling alone in my duplex, whiling away the hours on *Mega Man 3* again and again. When I grew bored of that, I re-watched *Angry Video Game Nerd* episodes until somebody in the comments section mentioned RetrowareTV.

Lance Cortez and John Delia, the co-founders of RetrowareTV, met in the mid-aughts at A&E. Cortez, a library assistant, and Delia, a supervisor of new media distribution, bonded over their love of not only retro video games but also television production. In a 2012 interview with fellow YouTuber Bryan Clark at MAGFest—an annual video game festival in DC—Delia revealed that the website got its start when "[Cortez] called me up and said, 'Why not do a series or show [about retro games] but make it a more serious take instead of just doing jokes?'" What emerged from those initial conversations was *Retroware: The Show*, an online video series housed at RetrowareTV.com that featured reviews, interviews, and retrospectives that used retro games as fertile ground for serious discussion. The content was more informative than academic, but *Retroware: The Show*—later expanded into an entire umbrella of retro-game-focused content—was one of the first counterpoints to the *Angry Video Game Nerd* that proved online shows about games could take themselves seriously.

RetrowareTV was the next old school game channel I discovered on the web after *AVGN*. It wasn't necessarily the first or biggest channel of its kind, but what RetrowareTV established—at least for me—was that the success of *Angry Video Game Nerd* wasn't a one-off venture wholly dependent on James Rolfe. Rather, the popularity of disparate shows like *Pat the NES Punk*, *The Completionist*, and *The Gaming Historian* prove there's a massive pool of people interested in older games like *Mega Man 3*. It was a revelation. I'd never met anyone else who collected retro games. Now I had proof I wasn't alone. What early adopters like Lance Cortez and John Delias might not have predicted, however, was just how much money there was to be made in retro gaming YouTube.

In the YouTube economy, ad views equal money. Estimates on how much video content creators make via YouTube ad revenue are hard to come by, and most retro game YouTubers are reluctant—and rightfully so—to disclose how much they make. Some websites like Business Insider suggest that a YouTuber makes $7.60 per 1000 views, while others say that's way off base. What we can be sure of, however, is that video production has allowed many creators to quit their day jobs and work full time on their brands via social media, conference appearances, and Patreon—an online platform where fans can pay for exclusive content. Felix Kjellberg, a Swedish-born 26-year-old otherwise known as PewDiePie, earned over seven million dollars in 2014 mostly for livestreaming games on YouTube and Twitch. His success is an outlier but hints at things to come in a media landscape where major TV networks struggle to get the attention of a cord-cutting millennial audience.

And yet, I'm troubled when I watch online videos about retro games. And trust me, I fall asleep almost every night to some random livestream of *Mega Man 3* or another NES classic—much to the chagrin of my eternally patient wife. My stomach turns sour when I finish one, the same way I felt in college after gorging myself at the Chinese buffet, the ensuing realization that I was my own worst enemy. What's propelling so many thirty-somethings to return to the trinkets of their childhood night after night? Why can't we all just move on? Maybe I'm just a curmudgeon. Maybe returning to *Mega Man 3* again and again is no different than reading *Pride and Prejudice* for the hundredth time. But when I watch videos about the Fairchild Channel-F or Neo Geo Pocket, I remember James Rolfe's proclamation in his behind-the-scenes *Angry Video Game Nerd* video: "Why would anyone bother to complain about a game that's so old, and why would they still be playing it? That's the whole joke."

None of us got the joke.

We're all his parodies.

•

Bad news awaits those who tackle Gemini Man third. His weapon—the coveted Gemini Laser—doesn't become helpful until the Dr. Wily levels much later in the game. In other *Mega Man* games, there's a clear one-through-eight pattern you can follow from beginning to end. In *Mega Man 3*, there are two cycles. Needle beats Snake beats Gemini, then Top beats Shadow beats Spark beats Magnet beats Hard. That's right. It's time to begin anew.

The Top Man level is one of the more straightforward in *Mega Man 3*. The player marches past flashing stadium lights and glass walls concealing dense pockets of lush foliage. There are no mid-level transformations, no organic fortresses, no convoluted mechanical snake paths. There is, however, one bizarre enemy patrolling the hallowed halls of Top Man's lair. Outlast the roaming Pickle Dozers—bulldozers driven by those hard hat-wearing yellow shits from pretty much every Mega Man game in existence—you'll find yourself in a small room protected by a robot tomcat that bears more than a healthy resemblance to Garfield. *Nintendo Power* refers to him as a Bobcat, and his main form of attack is hurling balls of yarn. Most of the enemies in *Mega Man 3* are thematically relevant to whichever Robot Master stalks the final room. Top Man's stage is patrolled by bulldozers and lasagna-fetishist feline robots. Re-equip the Search Snake and observe the David Lynchian horrors of robot snakes consuming a mechanical kitten whole. And if that isn't enough, go two rooms forward and find yet another Bobcat to feed to your minions.

•

Rockman 2: Dr. Wily no Nazo, or *Mystery of Dr. Wily*, began development at Capcom alongside *Pro Yakyuu? Satsujin Jiken!* Akira Kitamura and his second-in-command Keiji Inafune returned to the team and, with a development time of only three months, rushed to program the many features they intended to include in the original game. The original game's six Robot Masters were expanded to eight, and based on feedback from players, the dev team added three new support items—two types of flying platforms and a jet, the predecessors to Rush's abilities in *Mega Man 3*. Kitamura explained to Hitoshi Ariga:

> The enemies and the weapons are the core of Mega Man, so we thought about them a lot. Unfortunately, *MM1* and *MM2* really have a lot of rough spots. In *MM2* especially, we truly had no time. We hardly spent any time fine-tuning and polishing the bosses [...]. Normally we'd do a lot of playtesting, trying out all the weapons in different places... but in *MM2* we didn't do anything. Once something was finished, we'd check that it worked, and that was that. If we hadn't done it like that, we never would have made the deadline.

Luckily for them, Kitamura and Inafune did not have to develop all of the game's new characters alone. Kitamura staged a contest where children all across Japan could submit their own Robot Master designs, eight of which were inserted into the final game. Once again, Kitamura drew inspiration from Japanese hero shows. Inafune told J. W. Szczepaniak:

In the 1980s, many Sentai anime or manga like *Kinnikuman*, *Kamen Rider*, *kaiju* entertainment, and others would use magazines to conduct fan submission campaigns and solicit new monster designs from many different children and so on. I did that when I was a kid—I saw those things being run and even sent a few of my own ideas in. It was something that Japanese kids were all familiar with and participated in. We didn't invent the system, we didn't pioneer this idea. We simply took that as a hint, as an idea for something we wanted to do with *Mega Man*, and our aim was to have characters and bosses that we ourselves would have enjoyed as children. We wanted to get back to that sense of child-like excitement and wonder… We used to get 100,000 ideas, I think… People don't contribute a fully designed boss, they don't contribute a personally drawn sprite, or anything like that. They will send in their basic design and I will take the fundamentals of their idea and produce a boss from that.

Not everyone from the original *Mega Man* development team returned for the sequel. Manami Matsumae was promoted to the arcade division, and although she provided a few bars, most of *Mega Man 2*'s soundtrack was written by newcomer Takashi Tateishi fresh off the arcade racer *Mad Gear*. Credited in *Mega Man 2* as Ogeretsu Kun, Takashi Tateishi told Mohammed Taher—the creative director at Brave Wave, a music label focused on "the interplay between video games, music, and nostalgia"—in a 2016 interview on the label's website that he "was actually quite happy to be involved with *Mega Man 2*, as I loved the first game. But my first few attempts at creating songs were rejected by Kitamura-san for making music that sounded too cute. I was asked to make 'cooler' music. In fact, of all the songs I made in that first pass, only Crash Man made it into the final game." Kitamura told Ariga that "I was really worried when I heard his first songs. I was taken aback—they were extremely cutesy sounding, like something from *Bubble Bobble* or *Fantasy Zone*." In response, Tateishi moved away from the cutesy style in favor of rock music. "There weren't a lot of games with rock motifs at the time. If you look at *Super Mario*, that's more like classical music, right? So with *Mega Man 2* I did imagine as if the music would be played by a guitar… I'd make a song in the morning and Kitamura-san would approve it in the afternoon, and then the game data would exist that night." Again, Kitamura's insistence on perfection paid off. Tateishi's *Mega Man 2* soundtrack is considered by many to be the greatest video game soundtrack not just on the NES, but of all time. James Rolfe told me, "The [Mega Man soundtrack] that's stuck in my head is *2*, probably because it's the one we're all most familiar with. It's probably one of the best video game soundtracks ever." Search any of the songs on YouTube, and you'll discover dozens upon dozens of covers. Kitamura had at last found a composer he meshed with, and continued collaborating with Tateishi for the rest of his career.

In a 2004 interview with the now defunct *Play Magazine*, Inafune said of *Mega Man 2*'s development process:

> [W]e worked really, really hard, you know, just 20-hour days to complete this, because we were making something we wanted to make. Probably in all my years of actually being in a video game company, that was the best time of my working at Capcom, because we were actually working toward a goal, we were laying it all on the line, we were doing what we wanted to do. And it really showed in the game, because it's a game, once again, that we put all our time and effort and love, so to speak, into it, designing it. That's why that's my favorite [Mega Man] game, and that really established Mega Man as a series.

That passion paid off. *Mega Man 2* sold 1.51 million copies and remains the highest selling game in the series nearly two decades after its release. Capcom had at last achieved their dream of establishing a Famicom-exclusive phenomenon, and Mega Man's place as the company's mascot was fully cemented. A sequel was inevitable, but the tension between Akira Kitamura and Capcom was about to hit a fever pitch.

•

After you've killed two Bobcats and a Top Dispenser—a giant, red robot that shoots an infinite supply of spinning tops out of his stomach—you at last approach Top Man. This Robot Master has one pattern he sticks to even when flirting with death. He stands inert on one side of the room and fires away. Then he launches three spinning tops into the air before leaping to the other side of the room and repeating. Equip the Needle Cannon—a rapid fire version of your arm cannon— and hold the B button. Don't worry about dodging the Mega Man-seeking tops. This is a war of attrition, and when Top Man is felled and you are victorious, you are rewarded with another collectible, another item, more proof that you are becoming a better, truer, more idealized version of yourself.

In 2012, I landed a tenure-track job teaching English and creative writing in Indianapolis. The only problem was I had less than a hundred dollars in the bank, two maxed-out credit cards from a few years adjuncting, and relentless student loan debt carried over from grad school and undergrad. I still lived in Pittsburgh with two roommates and decided to move back with my parents for the summer to save money. I was 27 and fell asleep each night next to my sun-faded *Nintendo Power* poster from January 1991.

Thirteen years had passed since my old buddy Mike introduced me to Nesticle in high school, and in that time I'd managed to acquire over 200 NES games, 50 SNES games, and a few dozen others for the Atari 2600, Intellivision, and Nintendo 64. I owned bloated sets of PlayStation and Wii games, not to mention dusty *Pong* consoles and even a relatively useless Commodore Vic-20, a 1982 computer that resembled a typewriter. I didn't lug everything back to my eternally bankrupt hometown of Scranton, but I brought enough with me to sell. I needed money. And my first move beyond applying for additional credit cards and yet another loan was to auction off any retro items deemed non-essential. That list was embarrassingly short.

I was vaguely aware that some retro video games were worth legit money, but since I had never used eBay—where base prices were established—I was woefully misinformed. In pawnshops and flea markets, I rarely offered more than five dollars, and most times sellers were just happy to be rid of old junk that wasn't even theirs. In Scranton, however, I understood that if I wanted to make money, I needed to go online and discover fair prices for what I wanted to sell. That's how I finally stumbled across NintendoAge.

Founded in 2001, NintendoAge serves as the virtual town hall for the most serious NES collectors across the globe. At its heart is a vibrant forum with nearly 8,000 members and a comprehensive collection tool that allows us to track every NES game owned. In 2012, I still brought a six-page checklist with me every time I went out searching for NES games. NintendoAge put that list on a cellphone. More importantly, however, the site brings together the world's biggest NES collectors in one virtual space. Ideas, information, and auctions are shared, and in this way I learned of the price spike.

It's impossible to accurately place an objective value on a retro game just like it's impossible to truly nail down a price for a 1970s vinyl. Scarcity and demand vary depending on your location, and a pawnshop in Idaho might not cross-reference their prices with some nebulous online tool. The website Price Charting is the closest thing retro gaming has to a pricing standard. Aggregating sold prices from eBay, Amazon, and Half. com, Price Charting assigns a market value to games that fluctuates over time as supply and demand change. The good folks at NintendoAge suggested I use Price Charting to figure out what my collection might be worth, and what I learned was staggering. In 2008, the average price for a loose NES cartridge was $6.35. That fell in line with my experiences, and the algorithm even factored in expensive games like *DuckTales 2* or *Tengen Tetris*, which I'd seen in stores for $30 each. What stunned me was that by 2012, the average price had more than doubled to $13.06. That may not seem like a lot, but why would outdated pieces of technology suddenly double in cost nearly ten years after the NES was officially discontinued in North America?

I sold off some expensive PlayStation JRPGs until I was able to afford the upfront moving cost. But years after that strange, Scrantonian summer, I remain fascinated with Price Charting and the rapid uptick of NES prices. What I didn't realize then was that in four short years I'd look back on 2012 as the good old days. In 2016, the current value of your run-of-the-mill, loose NES cartridge is $23.34, nearly quadruple the 2008 average. More troubling is the sudden rise in rare game prices. The aforementioned *DuckTales 2*, which sold routinely for $28.99 in 2008, sells for $162.63 today. A version with the box, manual, and inserts will run you close to $400. Want that factory sealed? Then pony up $749 for a glorified paperweight.

DuckTales 2 isn't an outlier. As of 2016, there are now 39 different North American NES games that retail online for over $100. This goes beyond the uber-rare *Nintendo World Championship*—an unreleased contest cartridge that sells for $10,000. The price increase has even extended to games from the end of the NES' lifespan with low-production runs like the Blockbuster exclusive *Flintstones: Surprise at Dinosaur Peak* or *Little Samson*. The former sells for $1,876 in the box, the latter for $2,750 or $920 for a loose copy.

Even *Mega Man 3* has been affected. As one of the system's top 50 sellers, *Mega Man 3* is an extremely common game that fell to dirt-cheap prices when the NES became obsolete. In November 2007, *Mega Man 3*'s average price online was a mere $4.75, which meant it probably went for even less in flea markets and pawnshops. By February 2016, it sold for $23.99 loose. Boxed copies with the manual cost $72.98. Sealed copies have sold for $438.06.

This prompts two questions: (1) What caused the price jump? and (2) Who is actually willing to pay over $700 for something like *Cheetahmen II*, a glitchy unlicensed NES game that is literally unplayable after the fourth level?

As you might expect, NintendoAge is full of theories on both subjects, and while researching this book, I reached out to the site's users for opinions. A poster named The Bear phrased it this way: "People my age, a bit younger, and a bit older started getting jobs. The jobs got them money, and they dipped back into their past." Nearly every user I talked to brought up nostalgia and that the rise in NES prices coincided with folks born in the late 70s and early 80s gaining disposable income. Likewise, Mike Pellegrino wrote, "More and more people seem to get into this hobby every year but the supply doesn't change. There are no more old games being made. Whatever was produced is it." This is also true. If we assume most collectors are keeping their newly acquired games and factor in the inevitable cartridges that are destroyed after being unearthed in childhood basements and attics, that means there are fewer NES cartridges in circulation now than at any other point after the NES's heyday. More collectors plus fewer games equal higher prices. Mike Hodson tackled why there might be more retro collectors today than in years past: "I think prices are going up because of the lack of creativity in newer games." This is a commonly held belief among collectors that is difficult to asses.

But there is another culprit mentioned often by users on NintendoAge and other collector-focused forums. When asked what he attributed the price rise

to, the collector Fmdof wrote one word: "YouTube."
When asked what he thought of YouTube retro game
channels like *Angry Video Game Nerd* and *Pat the NES
Punk*, Fmdof explained:

> FUCKING HATE IT!!!!!!!!!!! Been bitching about
> it for years on here. It's a small part of killing the
> hobby. All these douche bags filming themselves
> in front of their collection, talking about rare
> expensive titles, has done nothing but fuel people
> to go buy said rare titles, film themselves and
> hope to achieve similar success to those others.

It might be surprising, but seemingly benign
YouTube channels like *Angry Video Game Nerd* or
JonTron are polarizing on NintendoAge. Many users,
like Moobox, aka Chris Hanratty, legitimately enjoy the
videos: "I think they are great! It's good entertainment
surrounding the world of retro gaming, something
which isn't available in mainstream media. The people
who create that content on YouTube seem to be enjoying
themselves, so that is really all that matters!" However,
others show open disdain for the entire YouTube
collecting community. Seora wrote, "It's a bunch of
crap. I won't even dwell on it." Surprisingly, many users,
even if they enjoy the content, blame the channels for
the price rise. Submissive421 claimed:

Youtube is probably one of the main reasons for high hikes. Media is constantly updated, so people can easily look up something and find the value. If somebody knows what it is worth they automatically try to make a quick buck. Games are readily available everywhere so it isn't hard to start a collection. People like Angry Video Game Nerd unintentionally caused decent titles to spike in price just by bringing awareness to certain games. Internet ruins everything...

Is YouTube really to blame? Episodes of *Angry Video Game Nerd* fluctuate between ten and three million, and 21 of *JonTron*'s videos have more than five million views each. But that kind of success is rare. *The Completionist*, one of the most popular YouTube gaming channels, only has four videos out of hundreds produced with more than a million views. The most watched videos of smaller channels like *Pat the NES Punk*, *The Gaming Historian*, *The Game Chasers*, or *Game Sack* generally range between 224,000 and 644,000. The most popular video from *Pushing Up Roses*, one of the few retro game channels operated by a woman, tops out at 170,000, but her second most-watched video sits just above 92,000.

Grouped together, can these videos really impact the price of NES carts? In March of 2015, NintendoAge user Marquidias hoped to find out by examining the effects of a video on *The Angry Video Game Nerd* channel produced by longtime *AVGN* collaborator Mike Matei. "Top 10 Obscure NES Gems with Mike Matei" was released in early 2012 and has since amassed 1.3 million views. In the 19-minute video, Matei details his favorite 10 obscure NES games in great detail. At the time of recording, the most expensive game covered—*Gun-Nac*—cost $40. The cheapest game—*Xexyz*—retailed on Price Charting for $2.41. The average cost of the ten games in May 2012 was $12.30. But by March 2015, the average had risen by $25.73. In that same amount of time, the average cost of an NES game only rose $8.01. Only one game on Matei's list—*Ghostbusters II*—dropped, falling from $6.80 in 2012 to $1.75 by 2015. *Felix the Cat* jumped from $14.86 to $43.78, *SCAT* went from $19.99 to $89.97, *Bucky O'Hare* moved from $22.12 to $74.58, and *Gun-Nac* skyrocketed from $40 to $112.50. The average price of an NES game was $12.44 at the time of recording and rose to $20.45 by March 2015, five dollars less than average price of the games on Matei's list. To me, that's enough to prove that major YouTube gaming channels like *Angry Video Game Nerd* sometimes raise the price of featured games. But James Rolfe, the Angry Video Game Nerd himself, isn't convinced.

When asked directly if his channel was causing the NES price rise, he told me, "I don't know. That's interesting. I think it makes sense that the older games get, the harder they are to find. Harder to find in good condition. Harder to find working… They just become rarer as time goes on, so they should get more expensive." When I showed him the stats for the games in Mike's video, he said:

It can only be that people selling them maybe saw the videos and thought, "I have that game, let me sell it." Maybe they're taking advantage of the videos when they come out, and it snowballs that way. I was talking to somebody the other day who told me he found [a copy of the game *Beauty and the Beast*] that went on eBay for $500, and I asked why it would be that much. It was because someone put it on eBay and asked for $500, and then someone wrote an article about it and said, "Look, *Beauty and the Beast* goes for $500." Then everybody else said, "I have that game. I'll sell it for $500." Then it becomes a bigger deal than it really is.

Maybe Rolfe's right. Maybe the rise in prices has little to do with actual retro gamers chomping at the bit to pay hundreds of dollars for unplayable disasters like

Caltron 6-in-1 or sealed copies of common games like *Mega Man 3*. Maybe it's online resellers and speculators, the same people who crashed the comics industry in the mid-to-late 90s, seizing hold of any opportunity to make money. Either way, what can't be denied is that every month the prices on Price Charting rise, a testament to how far people are willing to go to return to childhood.

What's a hundred dollars if it makes you feel okay again?

•

The opening screen of the Shadow Man level echoes *Mega Man 2*'s Quick Man stage. In that 8-bit gauntlet, you descend into an electronic cavern where every few seconds a white-hot laser screams across the screen. If the beam so much as grazes Mega Man's blue shell, you explode. The only way through is to memorize the pattern, a devious sestina of trial and error that surely caused its share rage quits. In Shadow Man's stage, you materialize atop two small cylinders, a waterfall of lava behind you. Your only choice is to leap blindly into the pit and face whatever challenges await.

For me, this is one of the game's quintessential moments—falling in front of lava, dispatching hopping robots. The fast-paced chorus hits as you reach the first

Pickle Dozer, and it makes you feel powerful and badass and good. Here in the Shadow Man stage, you truly feel like an acrobatic robot armed to the teeth, and it takes all my adult restraint not to fist pump while I plummet through the air.

Drop down past the Pickle Dozer, and Proto Man's whistle plays again. How you approach this encounter depends on the order you're playing the game. If, like me, you first encountered Proto Man in the Gemini Man stage, you might expect the cape-sporting Proto Man to toss an energy tank or aid your progress somehow. But if you attacked Magnet Man or Hard Man before Gemini Man, your first experience with Proto Man was a potentially deadly fight. Here in the Shadow Man stage, Proto Man ruthlessly attacks you, acting as though your friendly encounter atop Gemini Man's ice moon never happened.

•

Following the wild success of *Mega Man 2*, Akira Kitamura found himself at odds with his parent company. He'd managed to synthesize all his influences into one of the most memorable and beloved entries on the Famicom, not just in Japan, but across the entire world. And yet barely anyone outside the company knew his name. Only the most skilled players beat *Mega Man* or *Mega Man 2*, and even then they didn't see "Akira Kitamura" scroll across the screen—only his initials. Originally, Capcom hadn't even believed in *Rockman*, yet they received all the credit while Kitamura and his contemporaries toiled away in obscurity. Kiyoshi Utata, one of Kitamura's colleagues, had this to say about him in a never-before-translated interview from a Japanese fan publication:

Kitamura said that during the making of *Rockman*, the sales department people would really berate him, saying "Why the hell are you making this kind of original game?" In those days, when Capcom wasn't really making up original games, there were many games based on licensed properties like *Dokaben* [a baseball manga] or *Sweet Home* [a Japanese horror film], and when people would say that no one could sell original games or when the [executives] would insult him, he got extremely depressed. Sometimes he'd end up in the elevator with President Tsujimoto, who would say, "You're doing your best, huh?" and Kitamura would say earnestly, "Yes, I've been doing my best!" Then, after [*Rockman* and *Rockman 2*] the [executives] quickly changed their tune, all he could do was smile bitterly. It seems like that's when he started feeling a strong antipathy for Capcom.

Kitamura wasn't the only one growing frustrated with Capcom's restrictive corporate culture. Shinichi Yoshimoto, a designer for the popular *Ghouls 'n Ghosts*, was equally annoyed, and in 1988, the pair devised a plan to splinter off from Capcom to form a new company called Takeru that would put creators front and center. Soon they were joined by a dream team of industry veterans including frequent Kitamura collaborator and composer of *Mega Man 2*, Takashi Tateishi, the lead developer of arcade classic *Strider*, Koichi Yotsui, and aforementioned artist Kiyoshi Utata, who worked on Irem's unheralded NES gem, *Metal Storm*.

Things started off well for the upstarts. Kitamura's first Takeru game, *Cocoron*, a Japanese-only platformer for the Famicom, builds off many of the core principles established in the first two Mega Man games. Kitamura oversaw his own development team—the K2 Multi Creative Team—and the opening of *Cocoron* makes the differences between Takeru and Capcom abundantly clear. *Cocoron* begins with a credits scroll that uses real names, not pseudonyms, culminating with its director, Akira Kitamura. Utata said, "They had this sense that 'at Capcom they wouldn't put names on anything,' and rebounding from that was really a big thing. So that's why they put their names on the title screens. This was definitely due to a strong request by Kitamura and

Yotsui. In particular, even though Kitamura was the birth parent of *Rockman,* he wasn't valued at all."

In many ways, *Cocoron* functions as a shadow version of what *Mega Man 3* would have played like had Kitamura stayed with Capcom. You again play as a robot, but this time, instead of collecting weapons from fallen enemies, you're asked to build your avatar from an impressive library of parts at the game's outset. Want to combine a ghost head with a cyborg body and arm her with a baseball bat? No problem. How about a ninja face, boat chassis, and a deadly pencil for a weapon? You got it. From there, you're whisked off to a nonlinear stage select screen to begin your war against bosses proper. Your weapons can occasionally interact with the environment, and this, paired with the combination process at the start of the game, were both elements Kitamura hoped to include in *Mega Man 3. Cocoron* isn't the classic *Mega Man 3* is, but it is an echo, a variation on a theme. And although the game was never released in America, you can still play *Cocoron* in the US if you're determined. Head on over to RomHacking. net, and you can download an English translation of the game completed in 1999 by a hacker known in the fan community as Akujin. Everything old is new again.

Cocoron sold well for Takeru, but it suffered from being released eight years after the Famicom's debut in Japan and nearly a year after the technically superior

Super Famicom. Without the deep pockets of a massive corporation like Capcom, Takeru was susceptible to even small monetary setbacks, and, unfortunately, *Cocoron* would prove to be one of their few profitable games. *Strider* planner Koichi Yotsui directed *Nostalgia, 1907*—a cousin of Japanese visual novels or story-driven games like *Policenauts*—at Takeru shortly after *Cocoron*. But because of its animation and voice acting, *Nostalgia, 1907* could only be played on the Sharp X6800 (a high-end Japanese gaming PC) and the Mega Drive CD (Japan's Sega CD equivalent), both of which had miniscule user bases. The game was a flop that nearly bankrupted the company. In 1993, Takeru released their final game, *Little Samson*, a Famicom and NES underrated classic with mechanics that built off of *Cocoron* and *Mega Man 2*. Unfortunately, it bombed, and Takeru officially went out of business.

Many of Takeru's brightest stars escaped to rival company Mitchell, but not Akira Kitamura. Surprisingly, there is no information in English on what happened to Kitamura, the co-creator of Mega Man, after Takeru's demise. Type his name into Twitter or Reddit, and you'll discover all sorts of theories on his retirement or death. When former co-workers are asked about Kitamura, they'll usually change the subject or simply say he was/is an incredibly private person who wanted nothing to do with the spotlight occupied by

Keiji Inafune. When Brave Wave's Mohammed Taher asked Kitamura's frequent collaborator Takashi Tateishi if Kitamura continued in the industry, he said, "Takeru […] went out of business, and I haven't seen him since." When Hideki Kamiya—lead planner for the original *Resident Evil* and fierce defender of Kitamura's status as co-creator of Mega Man—was asked on Twitter whether he knew if Kitamura was still alive, he simply said no. When asked the same question again by a different user, Kamiya retweeted the question and publicly blocked the user—a warning to others.

I contacted Capcom of America directly for any information regarding Kitamura, but after they made initial inquiries with their Japanese counterparts, I was told they would be unable to help. I tried to ask Keiji Inafune directly about what happened to Kitamura post-1993, but when I sent my interview questions to his formerly enthusiastic staff, I was met with radio silence. Maybe Inafune got bogged down working on so many projects at once. Maybe their lack of response had nothing to do with Kitamura. Maybe Capcom really couldn't find anyone who worked at the company in the late-80s. *Maybe*. But the mystery of Akira Kitamura still looms large, especially, in the West where most *Mega Man* fans don't realize the titular character was co-created and didn't spawn fully formed from Keiji Inafune.

Thanks to the 2011 manga interview with Kitamura, we know he's alive, and we know that he permanently left the game industry following the collapse of Takeru. How he feels about Keiji Inafune becoming the global ambassador for Mega Man is unknown, although he left a clue in that 2011 interview. In Japan, Kitamura is often discussed as the parent who birthed Rockman, while Inafune is the adoptive father who raised him. The 2011 interview is followed by a brief, one-page essay penned by Kitamura for the manga's 2015 re-release. He claims that while he birthed Mega Man, *everyone* else raised him—all the programmers who worked on the various installments and spin-offs, not to mention all the fans. That *everyone* seems to be a subtle dig at Inafune's perceived ownership of the character and franchise. Takashi Tateishi, composer of *Mega Man 2* and *Cocoron*, doesn't think it's so cut and dried. When asked about Inafune's role in *Mega Man* and *Mega Man 2* by Mohammed Taher of Brave Wave, he said, "Kitamura-san directed the game but Inafune-san was the character designer, and he had a large say in how the characters moved, how they're designed and whatnot. So in that sense, Inafune-san can be credited as co-creator of Mega Man."

With or without Kitamura, Capcom wanted a new installment of Mega Man, and someone had to step in and direct the game. The obvious choice was Keiji

Inafune, but the upper brass at Capcom shocked the company when they went in another direction.

•

After your tango with Proto Man, you enter a long corridor—lava waterfalls bursting in the background— patrolled by enemies referred to by *Nintendo Power* as Holograms. These hovering, upside-down lightbulbs float across the top of the screen, occasionally turning the entire screen black. Luckily, there are no insta-kill pits of doom in this section. Even if the room goes dark, you can keep moving forward, firing Search Snakes blindly to clear a path.

At last, you'll stumble across Shadow Man, the fifth of eight Robot Masters. Curiously, his powers have nothing to do with shadows. Shadow Man wears a glimmering shuriken atop his forehead and dances across his lair, hurling those ancient weapons haphazardly. Equip the Top Spin and leap into the air. Hit B when you're above Shadow Man, and Mega Man will transform into a giant spinning top that literally drills a hole into Shadow Man's skull. Repeat four times and watch Shadow Man explode. Gird yourself for the road ahead.

III

W ITH A KIRA K ITAMURA DEPARTED to the ill-fated Takeru, Capcom selected not series veteran Keiji Inafune to helm *Mega Man 3*, but Masahiko Kurokawa, a talented programmer who'd paired well with Inafune on *Chip 'n Dale Rescue Rangers*. A grunt planner for the Famicom version of *Commando* in 1986, Kurokawa was promoted to lead planner the following year for *Higemaru Makaijima: Nanatsu no Shima Daibōken* or *Hell Island: Great Adventure of 7 Islands,* Capcom's attempt at a *Legend of Zelda*-style adventure game. *Hell Island* was a financial breakthrough for the company and remains so popular in Japan that it was ported to mobile phones in 2006. Kurokawa struck gold again in 1989 when he designed the home adaptation of arcade hit *Strider* for the NES. Luckily for Capcom, no one outside of the company knew exactly who Kurokawa was. Just like with Kitamura and Inafune, Capcom enforced its pseudonym policy on Kurokawa who chose the moniker Patariro. This wouldn't be the only time Masahiko Kurokawa played with pseudonyms. Later in life, he'd adopt the professional name Masayoshi Kurokawa, which was featured in the end credits of the underrated PlayStation classic *Tomba* long after the industry's pseudonym policies had fallen by the wayside. This has led to a great deal of confusion in the *Mega Man* fan community over whether or not Kurokawa's first name is Masahiko or Masayoshi, or if they're two separate people entirely.

Following the release of *Rockman 2*, Kitamura spent a lot of time pondering over how the narrative in the series had progressed. He realized that the first game contained virtually no motivation whatsoever until you reached the end of the game. Unless the player read the manual and discovered the brief backstory about Dr. Wily, she wouldn't even realize Wily was a character until she defeated the six Robot Masters and encountered him at game's end. This was a deliberate attempt on Kitamura's part to emulate *Super Mario Bros.*, a game with a villain and motivation—King Koopa kidnaps Princess Toadstool, and you have to rescue her—that doesn't explain its narrative at the outset. That game begins with a slow Goomba ambling toward the player, who realizes they must move forward to survive. Kitamura noted that only later does the player realize why they started the game in the first place.

For *Rockman 2*, Kitamura inverted that concept simply by including a subtitle—albeit one that only appeared in the Japanese version—*The Mystery of Dr. Wily*. By including that subtitle and including Dr. Wily's face in *Rockman 2*'s stage select screen—not to mention the text that runs in the opening attract sequence—Kitamura provided players with all the narrative justification they needed within the game itself.

Kitamura told Hitoshi Ariga, "When it was time for me to quit the company, I had a talk with Patariro, my successor for *Rockman 3*, about continuing the series [...], I was asked to give him any ideas for *Rockman* that I had at the time." Kitamura asked Kurokawa not to change any of the fundamental gameplay systems. More interestingly, he instructed Kurokawa to push the series even closer toward the soap opera aesthetic of his beloved Japanese ranger shows by introducing Proto Man and Rush, both riffs off characters from *Kikaider* and the Super Sentai Series. When asked directly by Hitoshi Ariga if he was the creator of Proto Man and Rush, Akira Kitamura admitted yes. Whether or not this means Kitamura actually sketched Proto Man and Rush is still unknown.

Even though Kitamura was departing the company to develop a robot platformer that would compete head-to-head with Capcom's Mega Man team, he desperately hoped the series would thrive under new leadership and provided Masahiko Kurokawa with some of his best ideas and concepts that would reinforce the foundation of the series—Proto Man, Rush, and a reliance on melodrama that would permeate the Mega Man X and Mega Man Legends series. As development for 1990's *Rockman 3: The End of Dr. Wily!?* ramped up, the series found itself in its most precarious position yet. Mega Man was known throughout Capcom as Akira Kitamura's personal project. Could it survive a changing of the guards? Would *Mega Man 3* mark the final entry in the series, or would Masahiko Kurokawa and the dev team prove that Mega Man was so strong a concept that a new team could design a fun game around the central character and established mechanics?

Unsurprisingly, Masahiko Kurokawa was not the only key replacement on *Mega Man 3*. Takashi Tateishi, the composer of *Mega Man 2*, quit along with Akira Kitamura to work on *Cocoron*, leaving Capcom in the undesirable position of having to find a third Mega Man composer in as many games. Once again, Capcom opted for a neophyte. Hailing from Fukuyama in the Hiroshima Prefecture, Yasuaki Fujita composed most of the tracks for *Mega Man 3* but was assisted by Harumi Fujita—no relation—just like Takashi Tateishi received help from Manami Matsumae on *Mega Man 2*. Harumi Fujita, a 29-year-old woman from Tondabayashi, Osaka, had already worked on the soundtracks for *1943*, *Bionic*

Commando, *Final Fight*, and Kurokawa's port of *Strider*. Although Harumi Fujita only contributed the Needle Man, Gemini Man, and Staff Roll songs and left the project during her maternity leave, the pairing of Fujitas worked so well they went on to collaborate with original *Mega Man* composer Manami Matsumae in Alph Lyla, an actual house band that performed inside Capcom headquarters sporadically throughout the 1990s.

The collaboration between Kurokawa and Inafune, however, was not a happy one. In many ways, *Mega Man 3* was a soft relaunch. The game's success or failure depended largely on Kurokawa's ability to mesh with the team members left behind from *Mega Man* and *Mega Man 2*. Unlike how candidly they'll discuss the first two games in the series, team members from *Mega Man 3* are reluctant to address its development process in English interviews. Keiji Inafune never refers to Masahiko Kurokawa by name, but we do know this: Halfway through development, Kurokawa abruptly left. The reasons remain unclear, but Kurokawa maintained a positive relationship with Capcom. He returned to serve as advisor on *Mega Man 5* and *6* and was the supervisor of 1996's mega-popular *Resident Evil*. The following year, he defected with another Capcom alum, Tokuro Fujiwara, to form Whoopee Camp, a short-lived game company that released two wonderful sidescrollers on the original PlayStation, *Tomba!* and *Tomba! 2: The Evil*

Swine Return. And the duo reunited to found yet another studio following the collapse of Whoopee Camp and released the well-reviewed *Extermination* and *Hungry Ghosts* on PlayStation 2. Unfortunately, that success was short-lived. While many sources mistakenly report that he has continued making games as recently as 2013, Masahiko Kurokawa died in July 2008.

Inafune is the most outspoken team member when it comes to *Mega Man 3* and Kurokawa's abrupt exodus, and, from his point of view, the development process was not a positive experience. When asked in Volume 220 of *Nintendo Power* in 2007 why he considered *Mega Man 3* one of his least-favorite Mega Man games, Inafune responded:

> The reason I said that was my least favorite wasn't because of gameplay or that I didn't like the game, but it was mainly because of just what was behind the release of the game. For example, I was forced to put the game out before I thought it was ready, and we lost the main planner [i.e. Masahiko Kurokawa] along the way, so I had to basically fill in that role to finish the game. I thought that we needed more time, and we had two months to finish the final 50 percent of the game. I knew that if we had more time to polish it, we could do a lot of things better, make it a better game,

but the company said that we needed to release it. The whole environment behind what went into the production of the game is what I least favored. Numbers one and two—I really wanted to make the games; I was so excited about them. Number three—it just turned out very different.

Even after leaving Capcom in 2010, Inafune rarely says anything negative about Capcom or his many years there. But in *Mega Man: Official Complete Works* Inafune spoke a little more freely without directly mentioning Kitamura or Kurokawa by name.

> We got a new leader for '3,' but [Masahiko Kurokawa] didn't really understand *Mega Man* the way [Akira Kitamura] did… and that resulted in some headaches. It was especially hard on me because I had learned so much while working on '1' and '2,' which left me with a lot of preset notions about how things should be.

Inafune took control of the team halfway through development, and by that time he felt only so much could be salvaged since Capcom refused to delay the release. From Capcom's point of view, they had to beat Kitamura and *Cocoron* to market.

Determined players can still find evidence that the game was rushed out the door. The Cutting Room Floor, a website dedicated to "unearthing and researching unused and cut content from video games," features a detailed expose on *Mega Man 3*. Hack deep enough into the *Mega Man 3* source code—something possible even for novices thanks to emulators like Nesticle and the proliferation of ROM files—and you'll discover tons of unused graphics, backgrounds, and even Proto Man animations that hint at vast swaths of unfinished content sealed off from the player in the final days of the game's development. The biggest piece of evidence, however, was not discovered by Millennial hackers, but by confused children in the 1980s who assumed they'd stumbled on the motherlode of cheats. Almost all game designers use a debug mode during development that allows them to wildly change the parameters of the game at will—adding more lives, more health, stopping time, etc. And *Mega Man 3*'s debug mode was activated by using the second controller, a peripheral otherwise unused in the game. In the race to release the game in Japan and North America before Christmas 1990, Inafune and company forgot to remove the debug mode. Play *Mega Man 3* on an NES today and hold right on the second controller to give Mega Man a mega jump allowing him to fly across the screen. Hold up and A and the logic timer will stop, freezing a number of enemies and animation sequences. These bizarre features are a testament to how much Inafune had to scramble following Kurokawa's sudden departure.

Like its predecessor, *Mega Man 3* was a huge hit financially and critically in both Japan and America. *Electronic Gaming Monthly*, then the critical bastion of games in the West, awarded the game 9 out of 10 points, but *Famitsu*—Japan's top gaming magazine— didn't rate it as highly as *Mega Man 2*. The game sold well over a million units in an age when console gaming was still in its relative infancy, and many of the staples established in *Mega Man 3*—Proto Man, Rush, and the slide—have been adopted in nearly every Mega Man game that has followed. Despite the dual exodus of both Akira Kitamura and Masahiro Kurokawa, *Mega Man 3* stands as the game that firmly cemented not only the Blue Bomber as Capcom's company mascot, but Keiji Inafune as the series's spiritual godfather. It once and for all proved the series could continue with or without Akira Kitamura, who was subsequently reduced to a historical footnote while Keiji Inafune ascended to the rarefied developer air reserved for pioneers like Shigeru Miyamoto and Hideo Kojima.

Mega Man 3 is the messy entry that should have failed and didn't. And despite the prevailing opinions of game journalists, message board users, or even Keiji Inafune himself, *Mega Man 3* is just as fun and noteworthy as its more famous predecessor. *Mega Man 2* was the first game in the series most people were exposed to, and isn't it possible that gamers automatically assume the best entry in the series is the one they experienced first? When it felt fresh and new and amazing? James Rolfe echoed this sentiment when he told me:

> [My favorite] was… *Mega Man 2.* I guess that's the first one most people played. I used to rent it from the video store for weekends. Then I started playing the other ones. I got to 3. When they were current, I didn't play 4, 5, or 6. 3 was enough for me. It was a trilogy. Mario made it to 3 [on the NES], why did Mega Man have to keep going? But way afterward, I went back and played them all. 3 had the slide. 4 had the charge beam. They always seemed to add something new to it. But for some reason 2's the one everyone comes back to all the time, including myself. I'm not sure why exactly that is. I think it's just that everyone played it. It came out at the right time […]. One time to be objective as possible […] I played all six *Mega Man* games […]. I beat one and moved right on to the next one. And as I got through it all, I remember talking to [Mike Matei] about it, and he said, "How were all those Mega Man games? They go downhill after 3, don't they?" I said, "I don't

know." To me they all seemed the same. They were all good. Maybe *5* and *6* weren't the best. But I thought they were all, as you said, interchangeable. They were all the same kind of deal.

And wouldn't that partly explain why I value *Mega Man 3* over *Mega Man 2*? I experienced *MM3* as a fresh-faced six-year-old. Nothing will ever again make me feel the way I did during that fabled weekend in 1991. I didn't even play *Mega Man 2* until high school, when I was busy listening to Slipknot in a Stone Cold Steve Austin t-shirt. By then, I was cynical and artificially jaded, my heart temporarily closed off from childhood wonder. My stubborn refusal to concede that *Mega Man 2* might be better than its sequel could be pure nostalgia.

The truth is the six Mega Man games on the NES are extremely close in quality, minor variations on a theme. The second game was a hit, the third close behind. That explains why most NES enthusiasts prefer one of those two over the rest: they experienced *Mega Man 2* or *3* first. By the time *Mega Man 4*, *5*, and *6* rolled around, most of the audience had already moved onto the Super Nintendo, Sega Genesis, maybe even the woefully underappreciated TurboGrafx-16. If that's true, then the "best" NES Mega Man game has less to do with content and everything to do with personal histories, thousands of stories like my weekend with *Nintendo Power* and a beloved Blockbuster rental.

•

Unlike most early platformer levels, the Spark Man stage provides the illusion of free will. The level begins with Mega Man beneath a platform housing a Peterchy—an eyeball with springs—and a ladder, and on your immediate left is an opening. If you're like me, you briefly wonder: Can I go back? Can I do things differently this time? The answer is no. This isn't *Braid*. Press forward into the zigzagging microcomputer comprising Spark Man's fortress and discover a litany of electric foes. One of the great player advantages in frantic NES games like *Mega Man 3* or *Life Force* is slowdown. When too many sprites enter the screen for the NES's 6502 processor to compute, everything slows to a sluggish chug—something Kitamura avoided in the first two Mega Man games by limiting the number of enemies on any particular screen. Spark Man's stage is full of slowdown, and you can use that to carefully stutter your way past whirling machines and eerie conveyor belts en route to the titular Robot Master himself.

•

To date, Capcom has released over 50 Mega Man games to the tune of 30 million sales worldwide. Many of those games are awful. In 1993, while Inafune's team was busy readying *Mega Man 6* for the nearly comatose NES market, Capcom farmed out the Blue Bomber to another internal team for the first time. The strange result was *Wily & Light's Rock Board: That's Paradise*, a Japanese-only Famicom game that's basically Monopoly with Mega Man characters. If you're hoping to play as Mega Man on one of the game's four boards, you'll be sorely disappointed. You can only play as Dr. Light, Dr. Wily, Roll, or one of two characters from the Russian-inspired *Mega Man 4*: Dr. Cossack and Kalinka. Inafune had this to say about *Wily & Light's Rock Board: That's Paradise* in the *Mega Man and Mega Man X Official Complete Works*: "The only things I did for this one were the package illustration and the design for the new character Reggae." It shows. Stripped of its Mega Man characters and iconography, the game would be no more fun than the lackluster port of Monopoly for the NES. The whole time you're playing it, you just wish you were playing a physical board game.

Equally bizarre is 1994's *Mega Man Soccer*, a Super Nintendo game that combines—you guessed it—soccer with Mega Man characters. Retailing in 2016 for $57—punting it toward the expensive end of the Super Nintendo library—*Mega Man Soccer* features what may be the craziest official description of any video game in history:

> A few months had passed since the battle with Dr. Cossack. One day, soccer fields all over the world were thrown into chaos! Familiar enemy robots restored by Dr. Wily were running out into the field and ruining soccer games. To deal with the emergency situation, Dr. Light modified Mega Man and sent him to make things right. "Go, Mega Man!! You must save soccer, and the dreams of those who love the sport!"

Let us also remember the oft-forgotten *Mega Man Battle & Chase*, a blatant *Mario Kart 64* clone for the original PlayStation released in 1997. The story justifications for why Mega Man's chosen to race his greatest foes in a Rush-themed go-kart are completely inexplicable. Pop in the game disc, and you're treated to the briefest of anime intros, in which a barely visible robot appears in outer space. The game jumps to a 16-bit cutscene of Duo—an alien robot who basically serves the Proto Man function in *Mega Man 8*—frowning while lighting flares in the background. Suddenly, the game switches to the jaggy polygons of the PlayStation, and we see Duo in a giant Corvette with what appears to be plane engines mounted atop the trunk. A heavy metal fanfare plays and the text "HARD GRANDEUR" flashes on the screen followed by "HERE COMES A GREAT MACHINE!" Then, after a brief loading screen, we're thrown into a 3D cutscene of Mega Man power-sliding a Rush/go-kart abomination around a canyon with Duo/HARD GRANDEUR hot on his tail. What other story justifications do you need? Although these excursions into new genres didn't fare well for the Blue Bomber, one genre where Mega Man translates surprisingly well is the fighting game.

Since the release of *Street Fighter II* in 1991, Capcom has been one of the biggest fighting game companies in the world. Over the years, Capcom has successfully developed a handful of other fighting series including the gothic horror *Darkstalkers*, the 3D *Rival Schools*, and many Marvel fighting games beginning with 1994's *X-Men: Children of the Atom*. The following year, Capcom attempted to spin Mega Man into his own fighting franchise with *Mega Man: The Power Battle* and again in 1996 with *Mega Man 2: The Power Fighters*. These two Japanese exclusives are the only entries in the franchise that were released in arcades. Both games allow players to choose from a roster comprised of Mega Man, Proto Man, Duo, and the sequel also includes Axl, a Mega Man X series character. Players battle one Robot Master after another, and although the presentation is similar to games like *Samurai Showdown* or *Mortal*

Kombat, the fighting feels closer to the NES series's boss encounters than the twitchy back-and-forth achieved in something like *Street Fighter Alpha 3*. Neither game was a smash hit—although they were ported to Neo Geo Pocket and later the GameCube, PlayStation 2, and Xbox as unlockable extras in the *Mega Man Anniversary Collection*—but they did pave the way for Mega Man and Proto Man to appear in future fighting game franchises including Marvel vs. Capcom and even Nintendo's Super Smash Bros.

Much like Mario with Nintendo or Sonic with Sega, Mega Man effectively served as Capcom's mascot for much of the 90s. Although he's been eclipsed by edgier brands like Resident Evil or Street Fighter that are refreshed with each new console generation, Mega Man remains one of gaming's most iconic characters. Look on Etsy, and you'll find over 1,000 unique Mega Man-related items. A Mega Man knit beanie? Of course. Proto Man constructed from a variety of neon beads? Absolutely. A framed painting of Mega Man battling Mecha Dragon from *Mega Man 2*? Yes, yes, a thousand times *yes*. Etsy overflows with Mega Man fan art and, when paired with the many bands directly spawned by the NES soundtracks, it's easy to see just how far-reaching the deceptively simple character has become. The hope Kitamura and Inafune shared while designing *Mega Man 2* in the middle of the night has been proven right. Just like Mario or Mickey Mouse, Mega Man is malleable enough to work in any number of narrative situations. He's going to live on.

•

The final obstacle in Spark Man's stage before the boss battle itself is an incredibly difficult stretch of elevators that rocket toward a spike-filled sky. Not only must you contend with the perennially rising elevators, but also the fearsome duo of Bolton and Nutton—vaguely evil nuts and bolts who merge Voltron-style. Your best bet is to never stop moving. Allowing Bolton and Nutton to combine when you're on a nearby platform is a recipe for instant death, and you want to conserve energy here because you can actually see the boss room where Spark Man is waiting. I'm ashamed to admit how many times I died mere inches from the door, like Moses collapsing moments before reaching the Promised Land.

I'm not exactly sure what Spark Man is supposed to be, but I really like him. His torso is this orange coil thing, and his hands are maybe cigarettes? Fireplace pokers? His head is a battery, and despite the dissonance of his body, he possesses a cartoony set of furrowed eyebrows like a classic Disney villain. It's the *Mega Man 3* design that most feels like it emerged fully formed from the mind of a child, thumbs blistered and hyped on sugar. Despite his amazing look, Spark Man falls easily. Stand next to him and spam the Shadow Blade as fast as you can. You'll take damage from his blasts of electricity, but the sawblades of darkness—this isn't literary flair: you're literally hurling shadow sawblades at the villain's coiled torso—will slice and dice Spark Man to death. The music fades to black. Your collection bloats.

•

After the commercial success of *Mega Man 2* and *3*, Keiji Inafune—having now solidified himself as the Mega Man guru following the exodus of Akira Kitamura and Masahiko Kurokawa—was given carte blanche to continue the series at his discretion. While other dev teams worked on the aforementioned spin-offs—not to mention a series of five Game Boy adaptations running from 1991 to 1994—Inafune's band of developers devoted the lion's share of their efforts to *Mega Man 4, 5,* and *6* for the NES and Famicom.

Released annually between 1991 and 1993, the so-called second trilogy of NES *Mega Man* games is often criticized for rehashing the same concepts from the first three games. This isn't unfair. Show a layperson random screens from the original *Mega Man* and *Mega Man 6*, and they'll hardly be able to notice the difference. Making matters worse was that by the time *Mega Man 4* launched in Japan, the Super Famicom had already been released. Gamers had already transitioned from 8-bit systems to the 16-bit ecosystem of the Super Nintendo, Sega Genesis, and TurboGrafx-16, yet Inafune's team toiled away on the ancient NES as it slid further into irrelevance.

Work began on an official SNES *Mega Man* in 1993, but Inafune and Capcom were not content to slap a new coat of paint on *Mega Man 6* and call it a day. In the *Mega Man and Mega Man X Official Complete Works*, Inafune wrote, "Now that we were into the Super NES era, we began talks about the possibility of a new Mega Man. We did a lot of brainstorming, trying to come up with stories and content." Inafune focused on moving the series away from Kitamura's upbeat ranger shows toward a darker, edgier tone more in line with the aging audience's expectations. In *The Untold History of Japanese Game Developers Volume 1*, Inafune explained:

When we were first developing *Rockman X*, Kitamura-san was already gone, so I took the lead. I wanted to take the opportunity to design a character I really liked, and make him the lead character. That character was Zero. I wanted a character who was Han Solo rather than Luke Skywalker. But if you make Han Solo, Luke still has to be the main character, right? So Rockman

X had to be the main character, but I gave Zero all the cool traits. Designing Rockman X was supposed to be my responsibility, because he's the lead character. But I gave that job to [Hayato Kaji] so I could focus on Zero.

Zero is basically a slightly darker Proto Man rip-off. Both are red and yellow with loads of radical 'tude, both are introduced as dangerous frenemies, both seem to sacrifice themselves at various points for Mega Man, and both eventually turn full babyface.

As development wore on, what emerged was a grittier game that still opts for the general structure of the beloved NES classics. This is going to offend some diehard fans of the Mega Man X series, but the story is a convoluted, second-rate anime mess. The game picks up a century after the original series, as a new scientist, Dr. Cain, discovers buried under some ruins a robot named Mega Man X—it's unclear whether this is supposed to be the Mega Man we remember or a new robot also designed by Dr. Light. Cain proceeds to mass-produce the Mega Man X technology, and enough of these new robots—inexplicably called reploids—turn evil that a squadron of Maverick Hunter robots is assembled to fight them. Their leader, Sigma, turns his team rogue at the start of the game and leads the reploids against Mega Man X and Cain. That's just the backstory for the first game, and unlike the original series, the plot twists and turns with each new installment. New to the formula is a sustained focus on upgrades beyond what you steal from bosses. Inafune explains:

> We were working on [*Mega Man X*] at a time when RPGs were exploding onto the market. The whole idea of experience points and additional powers according to your character's level was becoming mainstream. Then there was Mega Man, which was still a more classic representation of the action game genre. I started to feel that Mega Man was not shining as brightly in this light. That's why we wanted to bring in more power-ups. As far as weapons were concerned, Mega Man always had the "get new weapons by defeating enemies" system going, so we wanted to add another form of powering up. This train of thought led us to armor parts that enhance your character.

These small upgrades to the classic Mega Man formula paid off majorly when the game was released in January 1994 and sold more than 1.17 million copies. The gaming press heralded *Mega Man X* as a masterpiece, and *Electronic Gaming Monthly* awarded the spin-off a nine out of ten. The game remains a classic in Capcom's library and has since been ported to the PC, Wii, iOS, and Android, and was even remade with updated graphics and content for the PlayStation Portable in 2006.

Never shy about milking its properties, Capcom set to work immediately on a string of sequels continuing the ever-more convoluted saga of X, Zero, and Sigma, including one trilogy developed mainly for the Super Nintendo, another for the PlayStation, and two additional 3D sequels for the PlayStation 2. Meanwhile, the original Mega Man series continued as a kind of rebooted, kid-centric introduction to the *Mega Man* games in the form of *Mega Man 7* on the Super Nintendo and *Mega Man 8* on the PlayStation and Sega Saturn. This doesn't account for a series of Mega Man X side stories on the Game Boy Color and a Genesis update of the first three Mega Man games released in North America exclusively through the failed Sega Channel. What began as a quirky project envisioned by Akira Kitamura morphed into a full-blown corporate franchise with practically as many installments as the Super Mario games. The success of the Blue Bomber directly contributed to Keiji Inafune's meteoric rise through the company, and, by 1995, Inafune had already been promoted to higher-level planning and producing. Inafune was removed from the day-to-day operations of game development and tried his hand at upper-level management, far removed from the kind of work he did on the original *Mega Man*. It wasn't until 1997 that he returned to the development trenches to helm a third major spin-off intended to launch the character into the 32-bit generation, just as X had kicked off the 16-bit era.

The project began as *Mega Man Neo*, a radical reframing that would transition Mega Man away from two-dimensional sidescrolling into the boundless 3D worlds of the PlayStation. Inafune and his team punted the plot thousands of years into the future to a time when most of the Mega Man world is covered in water. Instead of a straight action game in the vein of the then-popular *Crash Bandicoot*, *Super Mario 64*, or *Tomb Raider*, *Mega Man Neo*—soon rebranded *Mega Man Legends*—pushed the JRPG elements of the X series even further. *Mega Man Legends* features a wide variety of armor and weapons for Mega Man to equip that affect his base stats and attributes in any number of ways. The game is a predecessor to current action-RPGs like the massively successful *Monster Hunter* series, but at the time, *Mega Man Legends*'s closest parallel was *Armored Core* or *The Legend of Zelda: Ocarina of Time*. Only *Mega Man Legends* wasn't nearly as fun or groundbreaking as those games. The story in *Mega Man Legends* is even more convoluted than the X series, and it features hours of recorded dialogue and cutscenes that break up the traditional town-dungeon-boss flow of most RPGs. The action, on the other hand, is a far cry from the frenetic pace of the NES and SNES classics. While sequels like *Super Mario 64* or *Metroid Prime* figured out how to transition classic 2D franchises into 3D spaces, *Mega Man Legends* falls into a more nebulous zone reserved for mediocre attempts like *Castlevania: Legacy of Darkness*. Both 3D games have the same trappings of the originals—whether they're robots or vampires—but neither game feels like its predecessors in tone or in mechanics. Despite spawning a direct sequel, a spin-off game, and a Japanese only PlayStation Portable re-release, *Mega Man Legends* didn't sell nearly as well as the original Mega Man or Mega Man X games, and represented the first legitimate crack in the franchise's armor. Side projects had sold poorly before, but never a main entry.

Keiji Inafune stayed away from the Mega Man franchise for nearly a decade, busying himself with the Onimusha and Dead Rising series, both of which were financial and critical hits. In 2005, Capcom promoted him to Senior Corporate Officer and later Global Head of Production. Away from the cramped development laboratories of lower-level Capcom, Inafune found himself drawn back to his first gaming love: Mega Man. Not the Legends incarnation, not the popular handheld Battle Network version, not even the techno-hardened warrior in the X series, but instead the original 8-bit

Mega Man. Did that version of Mega Man have a place in an era where the prevailing franchises were mostly North American first-person shooters? Was there still space for a quirky sidescroller like *Mega Man*? Inafune wasn't sure, but by 2008, he was ready to find out.

•

If you subscribe to the idiosyncratic and retrograde strategies of *Nintendo Power*, you'll select Magnet Man's stage first instead of seventh. It's not a terrible plan, but it's not a surefire hit either. The Magnet Man level is one of the shortest in the game, and many of its areas feel like tutorials to the game's newer concepts until you reach the boss. Early on, you drop into an underground cavern where you hear Proto Man's familiar whistle.

Nintendo Power frames the encounter in a curious way: "The mysterious Break Man means no real harm, although his weapon is real enough. He seems to want to train Mega Man for more formidable opponents. When he's had enough, he'll move on and open the passage." If, like *Nintendo Power* suggests, you tackle the Magnet Man stage first, this Proto Man bout serves as an introduction to all future Proto Man encounters. He whistles, runs from right to left, jumps once or twice, then disappears. Imagine if you received this game as a child in 1990. If you selected Magnet Man first, you might believe that Inafune and Capcom had thrown out the guidelines of the first two Mega Man games like Miyamoto and Nintendo did with *Super Mario Bros. 2* or *Zelda II: The Adventure of Link*. No longer did bosses wait at the end of the levels. Now they assaulted you at random. From here on, anything could be possible.

•

Keiji Inafune understood more than anyone how much had changed in the video game industry in the 21 years following the original *Mega Man*'s release. By 2008, video games had transformed from small projects dominated by three or four people that could be completed in a few months' time to an industry where one game could support hundreds of employees, years of development time, and millions upon millions of dollars in upfront costs. That sea change, spurred on by the massive processing power of nextgen systems like the Wii, Xbox 360, and PlayStation 3, had transformed Japan—once the behemoth of the game development world in the 1980s—into a network of smaller companies (with the exception of Nintendo) that produced fringe titles that rarely hit the kind of financial benchmarks achieved by North American franchises like the hyper-realistic and violent Grand Theft Auto or Call of Duty series. However, Nintendo, Microsoft, and Sony each established ecosystems of downloadable content in which users could buy smaller, cheaper games from independent developers who didn't have the resources of the so-called AAA companies like Electronic Arts or Ubisoft. Many of the indie games on platforms like Nintendo's WiiWare or Sony's PlayStation Network shared more in common with Mega Man than Madden, often foregoing the 3D effects of modern games for cartoony 8-bit visuals. As gamers who grew up on the Nintendo Entertainment System and Super Mario aged into their thirties, developers recognized a subset of the market eager to re-consume the experiences of their youth. No one understood this more than Keiji Inafune, eager to prove he was still relevant.

Bolstered by the success of WiiWare, Keiji Inafune enlisted Inti Creates, the Japanese dev team who'd worked on *Mega Man Zero* and *Mega Man ZX* for Game Boy Advance and Nintendo DS. With a team of over 20 developers, Inafune and Inti Creates began work on what would become *Mega Man 9*, the first core series Mega Man in over ten years. Its predecessor, *Mega Man 8*, released on the Sony PlayStation and Sega Saturn, retained the 2D look of the 16-bit *Mega Man 7* but also added graphical flairs only capable on 32-bit machines. The same would not be said of its sequel.

For *Mega Man 9*, Inafune, Capcom, and Inti Creates returned the series to its 8-bit roots. For all intents and purposes, *Mega Man 9* is an NES game released in 2008. The game is slightly too large memory-wise to fit on an actual NES cartridge, but beyond that, it looks and feels like an 8-bit game, right down to the flickering sprites and chiptune soundtrack produced by Ippo Yamada, a Capcom composer who'd been with the company since 1994's *Mega Man X2*.

Unlike *Mega Man Legends*, *Mega Man 9* proved a financial hit for Capcom. This led directly to 2010's *Mega Man 10*, another 8-bit styled sequel for the major download services. This time, however, Capcom and Inti Creates managed to assemble many of the franchise's most famous composers for the game's soundtrack. Manami Matsumae, the composer of the original *Mega Man* who'd butted heads decades earlier with Akira Kitamura, returned alongside Yasuaki Fujita, composer of *Mega Man 3*, and a host of Capcom alumni to provide an all-star soundtrack for what would prove to be the final core series entry for now. Even the promotional box art pays homage to the original *Mega Man*, featuring the grotesque Mega Man that graced the original's North American cover. Many reviewers, however, saw *Mega Man 10* as a blatant cash-in that added little to the formula established in *MM9*. James Rolfe, the Angry Video Game Nerd, told me, "[*Mega Man 9*] was really exciting because of the novelty of it. They did a classic *Mega Man* game! And it kind of closes the circle because there's *9*. But then they made *10*, and I thought, 'Really? They're doing it again now?' I played it for a little bit, but I didn't go as far with it as I did with *9*."

In terms of gameplay, *Mega Man 9* and *10* are sublime oases amid a desert of modern shooters and open-world *Assassin's Creed* knockoffs. But they also stubbornly refuse to acknowledge the ways the series has evolved since 1988. Neither game allows Mega Man to slide or charge his arm cannon, key features in *Mega Man 3* through *6* as well as the X series. Co-producer Hironobu Takeshita explained that this was because they view *Mega Man 9* as the true sequel to *Mega Man 2*—another reference to Inafune's low opinion of *MM3*. But it's not as if the game is completely frozen in time. *Mega Man 9* allows for downloadable content, continues you can earn from Dr. Light, and even the series's first-ever female Robot Master. *Mega Man 9* and *10* are both fun games sure to comfort any gamer who came of age in the halcyon 1980s, but they feel outdated compared to similar 2D adventures of the modern era like the transcendent *Shovel Knight*, *Fez*, or *Guacamelee!*, games that have merged retro sensibilities with the many improvements of the past two decades. Unfortunately, we'll never know whether or not Inafune and Inti Creates might have capitalized on those elements in another Mega Man sequel.

In the wake of *Mega Man 9* and *10*, Capcom announced two new Mega Man games aimed at fans old and new alike—*Mega Man Universe*, a *Super Mario Maker*-esque take on *Mega Man 2*, and *Mega Man Legends 3*. Unfortunately, neither of those games were ever finished, and, eight months after *Mega Man 10*'s release, Keiji Inafune left Capcom to form his own startup. Much like Akira Kitamura and Masahiko Kurokawa before him, Keiji Inafune was finally ready to strike out on his own.

•

Descend deeper into Magnet Man's stage, and you'll find no obstacles, no pitfalls of insta-doom. This lack of difficulty gives credence to *Nintendo Power*'s theory that this is supposed to be the opening level, even if that strategy has been debunked by the fan community in the 25 years since the game's release. One of the more difficult challenges comes at the halfway point, when you encounter the infamous disappearing block puzzles first introduced in the original *Mega Man*. In that game, pink blocks would suddenly appear and disappear in pre-set patterns, and it was up to the player to navigate those blinking mazes across vast expanses of sky and danger. One mistimed jump, and the player plummets to their death. The difficulty of those original puzzles is legendary, and when gamers toss around the term "Nintendo hard," the Ice Man and Elec Man levels in which they appear are often bandied as Exhibit A. However, *Mega Man 3* throws a decidedly wicked curve ball. You can opt to memorize the patterns and carefully navigate the multiple sets of disappearing blocks, or, if you already have the Rush Jet, you can simply ride your rocket pooch to the next section of the level.

Again, Capcom's 8-bit design proves oddly prophetic. In most NES games, there is a predetermined path toward victory. Take, for example, *Ninja Gaiden*. You can choose which enemies to slice-and-dice first, but your general strategy always remains the same—kill away anything that moves and power forward. The disappearing block puzzle in the Magnet Man stage, on the other hand, allows for multiple play styles and solutions, something gamers and academics have dubbed emergent play. You can think of this section as the precursor to so many of the Grand Theft Auto series's most compelling missions. At a Yakuza-controlled warehouse, for example, you can engage in a nasty shootout, or you can simply steal a tank from an army base and launch missiles at the warehouse until all the Yakuza are dead. Magnet Man's disappearing blocks are the 8-bit ancestors.

The disappearing blocks turn out to be more difficult than Magnet Man himself, a lame duck Robot Master who simply reels you in with his cartoonishly oversized magnet—just slide away—before firing at you from above. In a direct nod to Cut Man, he wears a magnet on his head. Blast him to hell with your newly acquired Spark Shock and collect the penultimate weapon, the Magnet Missile. You are nearly complete.

IV

THE HARD MAN STAGE BEGINS with a healthy dose of nightmare fuel. A gigantic robot bee carting a neon yellow honeycomb—the Have "Su" Bee—emerges from the left side of the screen. "Su" roughly translates to "nest" from Japanese, but why the localization staff chose to keep the original Japanese in quotes for the English version remains a mystery. Regardless, the Have "Su" Bee drops its honeycomb every time Mega Man approaches. When it shatters on the rock floor, a gaggle of smaller robot bees emerges. This is a particularly hard—not to mention frightening—opening, and it's extremely difficult to move beyond the legion of Have "Su" Bees without taking a modicum of damage. For the final Robot Master stage before confronting Wily himself, Hard Man and his henchmen put up a valiant fight.

Climb up into the heart of the mountainside and you'll run into the Returning Monkey, a robot primate who hangs from the ceiling. Why are they called Returning

Monkeys? According to the Mega Man Knowledge Base, they descend from the Monking—a formidable foe protecting Wood Man's stage in *Mega Man 2*—and are predecessors to the Monkikki, the banana-hurling robot pests of *Mega Man 5*. As you have no doubt guessed by now, the names of Mega Man enemies are given with little rhyme or reason. Regardless, the Returning Monkeys in *Mega Man 3* offer an intriguing procedural choice that ensures your fight with Hard Man will be an interesting one. Upon encountering a Returning Monkey, he will leap to the ceiling, usually out of range of your standard weapons. You can either: (a) run forward, allowing him to get the drop on you for considerable damage, (b) try to throw the Shadow Blade diagonally at the hard-to-hit robot; or (c) use the Magnet Missile, a homing weapon that will effortlessly kill the Returning Monkey in just a few hits. The problem is that Hard Man is most vulnerable to the Magnet Missile, so the player must choose. Should you fight Hard Man with low health but a vast supply of Magnet Missiles, or should you go in with full health knowing you'll have to switch to the regular cannon halfway through? I choose the latter, but that completely depends on your play style and how many lives and energy tanks you've amassed. With the endgame a mere half-level away, the Returning Monkeys provide you with one of the game's most compelling procedural choices.

•

After graduate school, I stumbled into teaching mostly by chance. I was lucky and picked up new fields as I taught, expanding from creative writing to composition to graphic novels to editing and publishing to, inevitably, game studies. I devoured the work of Ian Bogost, Janet Murray, and Nathan Altice and slowly began weaving those texts into my courses, beginning with the more mainstream Tom Bissell and working up to MIT's platform studies or dense compendiums like *The Video Game Theory Reader* and articles collected on Critical Distance, my favorite aggregator of online game theory. After taking a job in Minnesota with a focus on new media, I flew with three colleagues to the island of Victoria for the Digital Humanities Summer Institute. DHSI is a week-long gauntlet of courses, not to mention a gathering of professors and librarians who believe the internet could be used in classrooms for more than just Blackboard and Skype, that networked collaboration and online archives and even games might reshape education as radically as the printing press once did.

The conference was hosted by the University of Victoria, and when my cohort of four arrived on the wooded campus, we broke off for our respective courses. They'd chosen Feminist Digital Humanities, Sounds and Digital Humanities, and Digital Humanities Pedagogy.

I opted for Games for Digital Humanists, and wandered to my classroom curious about who I'd find inside. Who were these digital humans, and, like me, did they lug box after box of video games during each new move? Had they too erected miniature Nintendo shrines involving the Virtual Boy and R.O.B., Nintendo's failed 8-bit robot?

The digital humans were young. Of the fifteen students, only a handful were north of 35, and even the course's instructors were graduate students finishing their PhDs. Only half the room considered themselves gamers, and only one other participant was a collector like me. But what united us that week in Victoria and beyond was our shared belief that video games were worthy of academic study, and could be folded into the university classroom to teach everything from close reading to gender politics. During our brief time together, we played games about the transgender experience, PTSD, drone warfare, and poverty. We discussed the procedural rhetoric of *Zork* and *Browser Quest* and cheered so loudly during a *Super Mario Bros.* speedrun that a nearby session leader came over and complained—the academic equivalent of a brawl. And it was in this shared sense of enthusiasm and hope that I glimpsed the future. The professoriate was aging. I'd been teaching college courses for five years, had been on the tenure track for three. Even my senior colleagues had grown up with video games, and the stigma I'd once imagined—an ancient white man twirling his mustache and shouting that video games weren't academic before returning to his worn copy of *Ulysses* and crusty cigar—was eroding each year. When, over a few glasses of whiskey, I told a senior colleague about my hope to launch a games journal and maybe even a games research library, she didn't recoil in horror. She was excited and supportive.

It's been a year since my first trip to DHSI, and I just finished teaching a new course I'd been designing for years called "The Critical Discourse of Video Games." When I printed out the syllabus before the first day, it didn't just feel like the culmination of everything I've been working on since reading Ian Bogost or Janet Murray. It felt like the natural result of my entire life—all those trips to flea markets, all those hours spent in front of my NES—dating back to 1991, when I first paired my copy of *Nintendo Power* with a rented *Mega Man 3* cart. Viewed this way, the story behind *Mega Man 3* isn't just solely about the game or dev team or retro game collecting. It's my origin story too, of how I came to be.

•

Near the end of the Hard Man level, you meet Proto Man yet again. There's a raised platform in the middle of the room, and your crimson adversary will use that to his advantage, leaping about and making it difficult to get a straight shot off no matter where you stand. Inevitably, you'll roll into the Hard Man fight with either a significant loss of life or limited inventory of Magnet Missiles.

The battle with Hard Man is one of the harder fights in the game mostly due to your weakened state. If you chose to magnet the monkeys to death, you'll run out of ammo halfway through the battle. At this point, you need to memorize his pattern, much like you did with Needle Man at the very start of your campaign. Luckily, it's fairly recognizable. When Hard Man dives toward one side of the stage, you must jump in the air or you'll be stunned by a mild earthquake. He'll then fire two fists at you, both of which will boomerang back, inflicting more damage.

As a child, I assumed that if you beat the eight Robot Masters, you beat the game. This hypothesis went untested because my friends and I never got that far, no matter how many passwords we traded. What you discover when you defeat the initial Robot Masters is that not only is the game not over, but the difficulty increases exponentially. After defeating Hard Man, you return to the suddenly empty select screen. A beat passes, and identical beige robots refill the Spark Man, Needle Man, Gemini Man, and Shadow Man boxes. Mega Man's eyes stare out at you, and you're left with no other choice but to pick one.

It doesn't matter which boss you choose first since you already have all the weapons, so I usually go with Spark Man, a level that predicts the ROM hacks to come or even games like *NES Remix* or *Super Mario Maker* that depend upon strange reimaginings of friendly and familiar childhood play spaces. The four reskinned stages are far more difficult than what you've encountered before, but they're shorter, and before you know exactly how it happened, you stumble across an inert robot with exposed innards bearing a striking resemblance to Guts Man, one of the more popular Robot Masters from the original *Mega Man*. The game pauses as the flickering ghost of Metal Man, one of the Robot Masters from *Mega Man 2*, descends through the ceiling and takes control of the lifeless robot before you. There's no text, and upon witnessing this scene for the first time, you might interpret it the way I do. The soul of the vanquished Metal Man has returned for vengeance. *Nintendo Power* claims that the Guts Man clone is a character named Doc Robot with the ability to summon different Robot Master guises, but that feels like a cop-out. We see the flickering soul of Metal Man descend through the ceiling into a new mechanical shell.

It's a powerful ludic moment precisely because it's left up to the player's interpretation, and I choose to believe in ghostly revenge. Either way, I found this section so difficult I swung my arms after a particularly frustrating death and knocked lukewarm coffee all over my gym shorts, keyboard, rug, desk, and, most importantly, my 1991 issue of *Nintendo Power* with my sacred *Mega Man 3* strategy guide. I peeled off my shorts and sat nude in the sweltering summer heat. I cleaned my keyboard and desk as best I could, wringing the coffee from my mostly ruined issue of *Nintendo Power*. It felt strangely destined.

Revisiting foes from *Mega Man 2* has the same dopey charm of the third act of *Back to the Future II*, when Marty must return to the climax of the first film. There's something comforting about seeing the familiar in the most difficult stretch of the game. This is yet another reason why I adore *Mega Man 3* so much. Fans on the internet use the reappearance of the eight Robot Masters from *Mega Man 2* as proof that the third entry in the series is inferior, even in 1990 trading on the nostalgia of previous experiences. My argument is it gives you the best moments of *Mega Man 2*—the Robot Masters—in a new context. Now you can slide and experiment with eight new weapons. As a boy, I always wondered what it'd be like to run through the original *Super Mario Bros.* with the many power-up suits of *Super Mario 3*. *Mega Man 3* allows you to live that dream.

●

Following the release of *Mega Man 10* in 2010, Keiji Inafune found himself at a crossroads. Although his first return to the 8-bit well was positively received, *Mega Man 10* earned mixed reviews from critics and players. Was there still a place in the gaming world for old pros like Keiji Inafune? What about the mostly Japanese companies that produced sidescrolling classics like *Castlevania* or *Contra*?

Enter Kickstarter.

In the 1990s, no PC game designer outside of the boys at Id Software was as celebrated as LucasArts' Tim Schafer. He served as Project Leader on 1998's legendary *Grim Fandango*, a quirky point-and-click adventure following the exploits of an undead travel agent, not to mention his work on revolutionary games like *Day of the Tentacle*, *The Secret of Monkey Island*, and *Full Throttle*. The slow-paced and cerebral point-and-click adventures of the 80s and 90s play today like lovable relics from a bygone era. The genre still exists in 2016 but will likely never again dominate the sales charts like it did in its heyday. Schafer sensed this coming change early and, just a few days after Y2K, left LucasArts to found his own startup, Double Fine Productions, where he spent five years developing the experimental 3D platformer *Psychonauts* for the original Xbox.

Despite overwhelming praise from much of the gaming press, *Psychonauts* was a commercial failure. Double Fine's next game, 2009's *Brütal Legend*—a real-time strategy/action hybrid about heavy metal featuring funny man Jack Black—was also a well-reviewed but commercial flop. With the company and his personal reputation at stake, Schafer turned to an unlikely source for money for his next big game: crowdfunding. On February 9, 2012, Schafer announced a Kickstarter campaign for an untitled point-and-click adventure game in the style of LucasArts' 90s classics. Asking for a grand total of $400,000, Schafer promised a bevy of rewards to early-adopters including the finished game itself, an accompanying documentary and soundtrack, a dense art book, t-shirts, a place in the game's credits, and even lunch with the game's creators if you pledged $10,000. Let me be totally clear here. Schafer wasn't asking for money to publish a completed game. He wasn't asking for funds for a half-finished game. His game didn't even have a name yet, let alone concept art or a demo. Fans were given nothing beyond the promise of Schafer's reputation. He simply pitched a return to the 2D point-and-click games of old.

Double Fine generated over a million dollars within 24 hours and by the end of Kickstarter's 30-day fundraising cycle had earned $3.3 million.

The monetary success of what would go on to become Tim Schafer's *Broken Age* proves that gamers are eager to support developers if it means access to genres that have fallen to the wayside with the widespread ease of 3D engines. As *Broken Age* astounded the gaming press with its monetary windfall, both Capcom and Konami—stalwarts of the Japanese 2D tradition—transitioned away from 2D games and possibly dedicated console development altogether. Keiji Inafune saw the writing on the wall.

Like Akira Kitamura and Masahiko Kurokawa, Keiji Inafune left Capcom to start his own company, Comcept, in 2010. Similar to Takeru or Whoopee Camp, Comcept signaled a return to what made Inafune's earliest games popular. In *The Untold History of Japanese Game Developers Volume 1*, Inafune explained, "the success of Double Fine reinforced in us the belief that Kickstarter could work." After releasing a visual novel, *Sweet Fuse: At Your Side*, for the PlayStation Portable in 2012, Inafune and Comcept announced their next project via Kickstarter. The campaign video for *Mighty No. 9* opens with a camera scrolling up a building just like in the famous *Mega Man 2* intro. But it's not Mega Man waiting for us on the roof, it's Keiji Inafune in a royal blue shirt the same color as his adopted son. Over the next five-and-a-half minutes, Inafune visits game stores, signs cartridges, promises to reunite his old development team, and describes a new project that sounds an awful lot like *Mega Man*. *Mighty No. 9* is a sidescrolling game where you take control of a blue robot with a boy's face who fights eight evil robots. After each victory, you steal their weapon. There's even a red robot tweener of the Proto Man/Zero variety. Inafune asked the fans for $900,000. By the end of the month, he raised more than $3.8 million, topping Schafer's *Broken Age* haul.

Projects like *Mighty No. 9* and *Broken Age* have signaled a massive shift in the way retro creators approach game development. Instead of having to prove to a larger publisher that a market exists for a small game appealing to retro gamers, devs can now plead their case directly to fans. Koji Igarashi, one of Japan's most celebrated programmers, left Konami in 2014 and a year later launched a Kickstarter for *Bloodstained: Ritual of the Night*—a spiritual successor to *Castlevania*—that quickly earned $5.5 million. Even lesser-known developers are entering the Kickstarter arena. Playtonic Games—a company made of former Rare employees who developed *Banjo-Kazooie* and *Donkey Kong Country*—successfully kickstarted *Yooka-Laylee*, a $2.2-million-dollar game that picks up where *Banjo-Tooie* left off. Greg Johnson, co-creator of the Sega franchise *ToeJam & Earl*, managed to hold on to his IP rights after breaking from Sega in the early 2000s. In 2015, Johnson's new company

HumaNature Studios announced *ToeJam & Earl: Back in the Groove* on Kickstarter and earned over half a million dollars.

We're currently enjoying a golden age of retro 2D video games rivaling the 1980s, but it's not just the old masters returning from on high to deliver new 2D classics. Gamers my age who grew up on the NES are at last entering the industry and developing mainstream titles that refine the look and feel of the NES's greatest masterpieces. Yacht Club Games' *Shovel Knight* is a sidescrolling platformer that marries the *DuckTales* bouncing formula to the happy exploration of *Zelda II: The Adventure of Link*. Derek Yu's Indiana Jones-esque platformer *Spelunky* pushes the tough-as-nails difficulty of *Mega Man* to its limits. Even more impressive is young gaming auteur Phil Fish's *Fez*, a retro-styled game that evokes a legitimate sense of sadness and loss as you explore a lonely 8-bit universe that's literally falling apart. When asked about modern 8-bit-inspired games, James Rolfe told me:

I think it's really cool that every kind of game exists at the same time. Before, there was a void where they didn't make games like they used to. Now they do. You have options [...]. [Retro games are] quicker to pick up and play, and that's what I need. I don't have the time in my life to get involved, wait for the download to happen to play the game, then you have to install something else […]. Then finally you start the game and sit through all these cutscenes, and you're just waiting for the game to start. It's all too much for me. I don't have that time […]. For some reason, when something's in two dimensions, it just works better in my brain compared to three.

The spirit of the NES—a focus on two dimensions and difficulty, a resistance to bloated cutscenes, and a mantra of gameplay beyond all else—is alive and well in modern gaming. Even though games like Inafune's oft-delayed *Mighty No. 9* or Fish's *Fez* will never reach the commercial or cultural success of billion dollar franchises like Assassin's Creed or Guitar Hero, these 2D throwbacks prove now more than ever that the gaming industry has emulated the film industry. Properties like The Fast and the Furious, The Avengers, and Halo top the financial charts, but smaller, more personal projects like *Boyhood*, *Birdman*, and *Fez* still exist for those willing to venture beyond the multiplex and GameStop. NintendoAge hardliners criticizing the video game industry for straying too far away from its 8-bit roots are wrong. Those games exist and will always exist. They just might not be on cartridges.

The rules of *Mega Man 3* are tossed out the window the moment you defeat the fourth and final Doc Robot stage. You're suddenly kicked back to the stage select screen, only this time, Mega Man's unblinking visage is replaced with a hitherto unseen character's portrait: Break Man. It's Proto Man with a slim red visor pulled over his face. Why, after an entire game of messing with you, Proto Man decides now is a good time for a disguise, I cannot say. But there are subtle differences between your fight with Break Man and your previous encounters with Proto Man. For one thing, none of your collected weapons do any damage against Break Man. Maybe it's the visor? Essentially, every strategy you've honed and developed over the entire game is useless—foreshadowing the final battle ahead. You're stuck relying on your arm cannon once again, but if you can't easily defeat Break Man/Proto Man by now, you have no hope of completing Wily's Castle. Break Man's attacks are identical to Proto Man's. He hops from one edge of the stage to the other while firing wildly. As long as you haven't wasted time—and, more importantly, life—firing collected weapons, you'll easily win. But imagine yourself as a confused player in 1990, how long you'd fire your collected weapons, how many lives it would take before you realized your collection was worthless, meaningless, that you had to venture all the way back to the start, when you were young, blue, and innocent. Only naked can you defeat him.

What's your reward for defeating Break Man? The first dramatized cutscene in the entire game. It takes twelve levels and an extra boss fight before Inafune and Kurokawa finally deliver textual justifications for any of the robotic mayhem you've so far endured. Mega Man teleports to Dr. Light's lab, where the good doctor informs our hero: "Oh no! Right after we received the last element… Wiley [sic] ran off with Gamma!"

In 1990, your first reaction upon witnessing this strange dose of narrative was confusion. What are the elements? Who is Gamma? There's no mention of any elements and nothing about a mysterious Gamma in the manual. According to the *Mega Man and Mega Man X Official Complete Works*, "Dr. Wily began assisting Dr. Light in the creation of the giant robot 'Gamma' to serve the purposes of world peace. But just as it seemed that Gamma would be completed, disaster struck. Something was happening to the robots that had been harvesting energy sources for Gamma on far away planets! Mega Man's newest battle was about to begin!"

So. It's only after reading the *Mega Man and Mega Man X Official Complete Works*—the first version of which was published nearly twenty years after *Mega Man 3*'s release—that we fully grasp the game's narrative. Even the game's apparent MacGuffin—a giant robot named Gamma—isn't introduced until this cutscene. If one of my creative writing students turned in a story this flimsy, they'd face a pretty rough peer workshop. But in *Mega Man 3*, none of this matters. The clear and overwhelming lack of interest in narrative on the part of the developers just reinforces how little story matters in a platformer like *Mega Man* despite Kitamura's best attempts to bring the games closer in line to Japanese ranger shows. Each entry in the NES/Famicom series features an increasingly insane story, but that never interferes with the core gameplay, which is almost always identical. The early Mega Man games prioritize mechanics and fun over story. Gamma? Dr. Wily? Even Proto Man or Break Man? It doesn't matter. Move forward and survive: a ludic narrative as ancient as homo sapiens.

After Dr. Light's warning, you watch Dr. Wily pilot an orb-shaped spaceship to his castle, the front door a giant skull emblazoned with his logo. What follows are six mini-stages that once and for all separate Mega Man novices from true, battle-hardened masters. To this day, whenever I begin Wily's Castle, I'm filled with dread, my palms sweaty on the controller like a high schooler on a first date. This is fucking Wily, bro!

Even *Nintendo Power* abandons you in the game's final stages. After providing you with detailed maps for every screen of the game, the last two pages of the strategy guide are just a poorly rendered illustration of Wily's Castle pockmarked by a handful of screenshots from the final six levels. Now, you can find dozens of FAQs and JPEG maps on the internet, but if you made it this far in the 90s, you really were on your own.

Unfortunately, none of the levels in Wily's Castle feel particularly distinct. They play like slightly altered versions of what's come before, and before you can settle into a groove, you drop into a water tank for the area's first boss encounter. It's... pretty weird. The floor and walls are made of cannons that shoot underwater tornadoes at you. At the top of the screen is a giant claw lifted from an arcade redemption game that dumps menacing turtle bots into the churning waters. After Shadow Blading five of them, the claw explodes, and you advance to the next level.

The second stage is even shorter than the first. Two-thirds of it are comprised of rooms where you stock up on power-ups, which you'll need now more than ever. Before Wily's Castle, your depleted weapons automatically refilled between stages. That's no longer the case, and you must carefully monitor your weapon usage—and, more importantly, the Rush items— throughout all of Wily's Castle. Run out of a needed weapon on a boss fight or Rush Jet fuel when you have to make an impossible jump, and you're basically finished. Level two allows you to restock only your most-used items. Choose carefully and quickly, as you'll be pursued through much of this level by legions of robot bees as you pilot your Rush Jet over one chasm of spikes after another.

One of the most notorious encounters in the entire Mega Man series is the Yellow Devil, a boss from the first game where a giant monster shoots its body parts at you at near-hemorrhage inducing speeds. In that game, players discovered a glitch where they could fire Elec Man's Thunder Beam, wait for it to hit the creature's eye, then rapidly pause and unpause the game. Each pause causes the game to register a new hit on the Yellow Devil for as long as the Thunder Beam passes through the monster's eye, allowing gamers to cheat their way through an otherwise insanely difficult battle. Akira Kitamura recognized the unfair difficulty of the Yellow Devil battle and didn't include him—or anything even remotely that hard—in *Mega Man 2*. But *Mega Man 3*, unfortunately, introduces the Yellow Devil Mk. II, a slightly easier battle that removes the Thunder Beam glitch. Ironically enough, the Spark Shock—the *Mega Man 3* equivalent of the Thunder Beam—doesn't damage the new-and-improved Yellow Devil Mk. II.

The slide makes the fight easier, however, and the Yellow Devil Mk. II hurls his body parts slightly slower than the original model—why Dr. Wily would produce an inferior model of one of his robots is never explained.

But if you've made it this far, almost nothing can stop you. Not even a do-over bout with one of the series's most fearsome villains. The end is at last within sight.

•

Even though many indie games take direct inspiration from the 8-bit era—*Mighty No. 9*, *Broforce*, and *Undertale* to name only a few—what will happen to the actual NES games from the 1980s? Already it's difficult to find an HDTV with the correct inputs for a Nintendo Entertainment System. What will it be like twenty years from now? How about a hundred? Will we repeat the mistakes of the film industry, discarding many of our early artifacts, or are there outside-of-the-box solutions?

Luckily for gamers past, present, and future, a number of organizations big and small are already working towards preserving games for future generations, much like the librarians and historians who came before them. Many would argue that emulators are the surest bet for preservation, as digital copies of physical media can simply be transferred from one operating system to another, in perpetuity, for as long as humans continue to use machines. But surprisingly, academia has opted for a more comprehensive approach. Kyoto's Ritsumeikan University started its NES archive project in 1998. Spearheaded by Professor Koichi Hosoi, Ritsumeikan's archival division has spent close to twenty years buying up every Japanese Famicom release, amassing over 1,300 games. Hosoi has overseen the development of his own emulation system that not only records each play session for future research, but also maps each button press so scholars can trace how exactly gameplay styles differ across populations.

Although Japan has been at the forefront of academia's video game preservation movement, more and more American institutions are joining in as gamers who grew up on the NES have aged into the tenure-track. The University of Mary Washington, for example, runs The Console Living Room, a stunning recreation of a 1985 gaming-centric living room, straight on down to the faux-wood paneling and shag carpet. There, millennial students can play *Super Mario Bros.* as it was intended to be experienced—on a crappy dial TV while listening to records. The University of Arizona, the University of Colorado Boulder, and the University of Maryland each feature Ritsumeikan-esque libraries of older consoles and games, and the National Museum of Play in Rochester, New York, features a staggering collection totaling 250 arcade games, hundreds of consoles, 35,000 home video games, and full company collections of rare materials donated by Atari, Microsoft, and Broderbund. Even James Rolfe, the Angry Video Game Nerd, thinks of his game collection as more than just a collection: "I think of myself as a preservationist […] By making videos, showing them, other people can see it. I love finding things I never heard of, because if I didn't, probably other people never heard of it either. Otherwise, it's just forgotten in time."

But while there are a few major organizations working on preserving video games for future generations, what do you do if you want to show your child *Mega Man 3* and you don't own a working NES or live near one of the aforementioned institutions? In 2004, Capcom released the first eight core series Mega Man games on a compilation disc—the *Mega Man Anniversary Collection*—for PlayStation 2, GameCube, and then the original Xbox the following year. Many older studios followed suit, and the PlayStation 2 in particular is a gold mine for Capcom, Sega, SNK, and Taito compilations among others. But the true digital revolution began with Nintendo's Wii in 2006. Much like how WiiWare and PSN cleared the path for indie developers to gain widespread access to gamers, downloadable services provided incentive for older game studios to release their backlog digitally. Nintendo's Virtual Console on the Wii and Wii U features dozens of classics ranging from any number of Nintendo and non-Nintendo systems that gamers can download for just a few bucks a pop. The Mega Man series is no different. While writing this book, I've kept a 3DS—Nintendo's most recent handheld—loaded with *Mega Man 3* on my desk at all times. I've also played the *Anniversary Collection* version, the downloadable PSN version on PlayStation 3, and of course, the original *Mega Man 3* on my NES.

But each of the new versions features slight modifications that differ from the original experience of playing it on an NES and CRTV. The PlayStation 2 and PlayStation 3 versions allow for an automatic fire option, and the 3DS version allows you to save anywhere, both of which render the game significantly easier. The PlayStation 3 version is actually a downloadable version of a Japanese-only PlayStation re-release of *Rockman 3*, so that means the game's "new" menu is completely in Japanese and that Mega Man is referred to as Rockman— oddly enough in English—throughout. And of course, you can't discount the effect of playing an NES game not on a simplistic NES controller and bulky television, but with a modern controller and HDTV. It's not better or worse, but it alters the experience, the same as moving from a hardcover copy of *Madame Bovary* to a paperback version of a different translation. It's essentially the same, but fundamentally altered.

Instead of porting slightly changed games to emulators or newer and newer systems, game studio Digital Eclipse is taking another approach. Focused on accuracy, context, presentation, and sustainability, Digital Eclipse is attempting to become the Criterion

Collection for video games. Their latest project, the *Mega Man Legacy Collection*, is helmed by Head of Restoration Frank Cifaldi and promises to go far beyond the aforementioned re-releases and updates. All six of the original *Mega Man* games have been re-digitized and upscaled for 1080p resolution for the first time. The *Legacy Collection* also offers NES graphical modes that even replicate slowdown and sprite flickering—a known issue with the NES's Picture Processing Unit where sprites flicker if too many are onscreen at any one time. Much like a special edition DVD release, the *Legacy Collection* also features a number of behind-the-scenes promotional art pieces drawn by Inafune and other Capcom stalwarts.

Whether or not Digital Eclipse actually will become the Criterion Collection of video games remains to be seen. What we know for a fact, however, is that fewer and fewer people will have access to an NES, CRTV, and original games each year. We can either act now and try to preserve as many as we can or suffer the same fate of the early film industry which was unable to protect so many of its earliest movies for future generations.

•

The third Dr. Wily level features one of the most interesting boss fights in the entire game. Taking a page directly from

Zelda II's Shadow Link playbook, the third Wily level concludes with a showdown with yourself. You enter a room with three Mega Men. Two are holograms, one is real, and it's up to you to figure out which one to murder. Here, you're confronted with a number of compelling questions. Are these Mega Men similar to the clone Mega Man from Wily's Castle in the first game? Did Dr. Wily construct a new batch of evil Mega Men, or are these left over from when Dr. Light originally built Mega Man? And if so, what separates you from them besides Dr. Wily flipping a switch from good to evil? The game provides no answers. The subdued darkness of this scene is for me only amplified by the passage of time, my slow mutation from a child exploring a game to an adult consuming nostalgia, grimacing through bourbon sweats.

The fourth Wily level features a staple of so many 8-bit and 16-bit classics. You enter a room of eight elevators, each one returning you to one of the eight Robot Masters you spent the first half of the game defeating. That's right. You have to fight all of them again, and this time you don't recover full health and energy after each victory. Otherwise, each fight is exactly the same. If the Magnet Missile worked against Hard Man the first time, it'll work here. The Robot Masters have learned nothing.

The boss rush segment of the game continues in the next stage when you at last confront Dr. Wily head on.

The villain finally scrambles onto the stage in a giant mechanical crab known officially as Wily Machine #3 (Form 1). You can't see his face, but his two weak points are his robot dick blasting globs of orange semen and his pink shielded cockpit. The background turns black when the Wily Machine appears, a cunning programming tactic on Capcom's part. The boss sprite is too large for the NES's PPU to process, so the developers cheated and added a moving background to the sprite to make it appear larger. To the player, this makes no visual difference. It's simply a large boss. But the NES thinks it's rendering a few smaller sprites atop a scrolling background—like the clouds in *Super Mario Bros*. It's a commonly used trick in later NES games and illustrates how the massive constraints of the 6502 processor inspired creative solutions.

To defeat the Wily Machine's first form, you simply stand on the left side of the screen and blast its dick off with a few well-timed Spark Shocks. The cockpit shielding explodes, and revealed is Dr. Wily and, more importantly, the second phase of the Wily fight. The Wily Machine's new form is exactly the same as the last, but now you can see Dr. Wily at the crab's controls. When the battle resumes, simply fly into the air with the Rush Jet and shoot at Wily until the crab blows up, sending Wily to the floor to beg forgiveness just like in *Mega Man* and *Mega Man 2*. Only this time, the credits don't start rolling. Mega Man will approach Dr. Wily only for his head to flop around on a spring. The Wily Machine was controlled by a toy!

The game kicks you back to the map screen, and a new final boss icon appears next to the one you just defeated. The stage begins, and you find yourself in a room outfitted with an extra life, energy tank, and a few other random power-ups. Then you descend into a pit for the game's true final encounter: Gamma.

It's stunning how easy the final boss is. Gamma, the giant peace-keeping robot first mentioned near the end of the game, is an enormous screen-filling machine with a face on top of another face that shoots lasers at you. There's a precise method of defeating Gamma, and much of the battle—if you're not consulting an online FAQ—consists of flailing around, searching for something that might hurt him. Very few of your weapons do any damage, and until you realize you have to stand beneath him and hurl Shadow Blades straight up—or Rush Jet to a girder to fire some Hard Knuckles—you'll simply take hit after hit and grow frustrated. Once you figure out how to harm Gamma, his smaller face will blow off, and Dr. Wily will descend in a robot Viking hat thing. Another metal girder appears on the right, and once again the player is left scrambling to figure out which weapon actually works. There's no challenge in learning Gamma's pattern—the chief difficulty you've come to expect in literally every other boss encounter. Instead, the focus is on selecting the only weapon that harms him—in this case the Top Spin—and realizing you must Rush Coil to the top-most girder and then Top Spin Gamma in the face. That's all it takes. One Top Spin and the mighty peace-keeping Gamma explodes. In terms of overall difficulty, the Gamma fight is far easier than any Robot Master encounter in the game and is honestly less difficult than some of the brief Proto Man battles. Even if you can't figure it out, you're simply booted back to the start of the stage. It doesn't make much sense why Capcom would craft such a difficult game only to top it off with one of the easiest final boss fights in not just the series but across the entire NES library. All you can do is chalk it up to the turbulent development cycle and Inafune's promises that he'd do many things differently if given the chance.

The ending, on the other hand, takes some artistic liberties. Wily is hurled from the exploding Gamma, and—just like in the first two Mega Man games and even the previous stage—grovels at your feet. In previous games, the scene shifted to the credits, implying that Mega Man turned Wily over to the authorities. But in the third game, before Mega Man can return Wily to whatever police force reigns supreme in the future, Wily's fortress starts to collapse and falling debris knocks out Mega Man and Wily. The game momentarily flirts with an *Empire Strikes Back*-esque cliffhanger, but before you can buy in, a shadowed Proto Man appears and kicks the debris covering Mega Man to pieces. He then leaps over to Wily and delivers this poorly translated gem: "Where's Dr. Wiley?... Oh no, too late."

What's the implication? That Proto Man has uncovered Wily's corpse crushed by cement? It's vague and darker than most NES games outside the Ninja Gaiden trilogy, but the player is given no time to dwell. "Epilogue" flashes on the screen, and we're back in Light's lab, the good doctor informing Mega Man he found him there unconscious. After the two wonder aloud about who might have saved Mega Man from the wreckage of Wily's lab, the iconic Proto Man whistle plays. Just like Kikaider's trumpet, the music here is diegetic as Light comments on it and guesses it must have been Proto Man. We smash cut to Mega Man running through the woods—presumably searching for Proto Man—as Dr. Light's notebook flips across the bottom half of the screen. Each page reveals another robot designed by Dr. Light—mistranslated here as Dr. Right—beginning with the six Robot Masters from the original *Mega Man*. Then we see Roll and Mega Man, listed as the second and first robots created by Light. And then, at long last, we get the swerve: "No. 000 Proto Man, New robot prototype, brother of Mega Man." Proto Man is Mega Man's brother! Mega Man stops running and gazes up into the sky. Proto Man's face is revealed blue and Mufasa-esque, as Dr. Wily's spaceship hovers in the distance.

The player can clearly deduce that Wily survived the destruction of his fortress and will appear in the inevitable sequel. But what about Proto Man? Why does his face appear like a ghost in the game's final moments before cutting to the credits? Obviously, we know now that Proto Man appears again and again. But in 1990, you might assume that Proto Man died saving his purer, better brother. You might assume that the blue outline of Proto Man's face was not foreshadowing for future video games, but a ghost, a grim allusion to the flawed character seeking redemption via sacrifice. When compared to the by-the-numbers endings of the first two games and the campy insanity of *Mega Man 4–6*, the downbeat conclusion of *Mega Man 3* is a success even if Keiji Inafune is ashamed of it, even if it never receives the credit of its brother, *Mega Man 2*. That game is about perfection, expertly crafted but devoid of quirks. But I love *Mega Man 3* more. Even if none of its creators think so, *Mega Man 3* is the slipshod masterpiece that veers headlong into its flaws and messy, unchecked ambition. The allure of its mechanical world—the last in the franchise colored by the direct influence of Akira Kitamura—is part of the reason why I keep my NES plugged in decades later, why I still scour yard sales and thrift shops and now even eBay for forgotten gray cartridges. I just want a taste of what it felt like when I was young and the world was new.

•

In 2012, I was often alone. I traded Pennsylvania for Indiana and left my family, friends, and my soon-to-be-wife behind. I knew no one beside my older co-workers and spent most weekends in an anxious blur, retreating to my NES collection and the same virtual worlds I'd hidden in my entire life. My games were a neon shield, a stubborn denial of the material world.

As that lonely fall dragged on, I became obsessed with the presidential election, just like I had eight years earlier, when I literally worried myself into palpitations and a heart monitor. Even though the final result was barely in doubt, I was sweaty and pacing an hour before the first debate, the black tendrils of anxiety reaching up from my stomach and into my throat. I wandered to my shelves of NES games and found that friend of my youth, *Mega Man 3*, the Blue Bomber happily firing a laser on the cover, reminding me of that Blockbuster weekend so long ago, when I was happy and excitable, the future aglow with possibilities.

One of my secret shames was that I'd never beaten an NES Mega Man. I defeated *Mega Man Legends* in eighth grade, but the core series eluded me no matter how many times I rented those menacing gray cartridges from the now-defunct Blockbuster. I tried again in college when the first eight games were repackaged in the *Mega Man Anniversary Collection* and made it to Wily's Castle in each of the first three games. But I never actually managed to defeat the evil Wily himself. Instead, each attempt ended with me hurling my controller and retreating to the townie bar for a fortifying draft of lukewarm Yuengling. I didn't think I'd finally beat *Mega Man 3* that night in Indianapolis—the debate was less than an hour away—but I wanted to burrow back to the 8-bit and two dimensions, a respite in an age of potential destruction—global warming, nuclear fallout, economic collapse, uprising, viral pandemics! It would take me decades to collect every last NES game, and it would take me decades to finally witness the ending of *Mega Man 3*. It felt weirdly appropriate.

I pulled up the boss order on my cracked Blackberry and was shocked at how easily I sailed past Needle Man, Snake Man, Gemini Man. I was already two beers in when I started, and, by the time the debate began, I was deep into my fourth. I drilled down into my drunken sweet spot and decided to play a little longer, to join the debate ten or twenty minutes in.

But then thirty minutes passed. Then an hour. Then another. I cleared the eight Robot Masters, then the resurrected bosses from *Mega Man 2*. I blitzed the Yellow Devil, and then, unbelievably, each form of Wily himself. I dropped to my knees in front of my dusty CRTV as the credits scrolled by and snapped a photo on my phone, proof that I'd finally bested the beast, that this was no mere fever dream conjured up by acid reflux and apocalyptic fretting. I swiped to Facebook and uploaded the picture as a Life Event. I wrote a semi-ironic caption, but the truth was it really did feel like an achievement. Eight years had passed since I started collecting NES games. Twenty-two since I first rented *Mega Man 3*. Twenty-two years with this game, and it culminated with a staff roll just like any other, Akira Kitamura's pseudonym already scrubbed from the credits. My NES was warm to the touch, and I was unsure if I should feel proud or humiliated that I'd spent a presidential debate beating a game from 1990, that I'd surrounded myself with hundreds of NES games and dozens more for the TurboGrafx-16 and 32X and so many other outdated and dusty machines.

The truth is that I don't know why I collect old video games or why I'm obsessed with them. But I do know this. We—the collectors of old silicon, the usernames who post picture after picture of games on NintendoAge, the sulking figures haunting flea markets and pawnshops for glimpses into our past—are looking for something beyond the tangible. Each instruction manual collected, each game shelved, each YouTube clip about *Mega Man* produced or consumed, temporarily fills some unarticulated need, some deep desire to be comforted or even completed. But most people feel incomplete or scared in some fundamental way. We live in a constant state of distraction, and that's reflected in nearly every collection or hobby people can dream up. The Nintendo Entertainment System isn't a time machine to a specific year or place—it's a telescope trained on earlier versions of ourselves, before the world taught us to be frightened of the future, the nightmare of 200X.

NOTES

Manga artist Hitoshi Ariga's interview with Akira Kitamura was conducted in 2011 and was published for the first time in volume 1 of the manga collection *Shinsōban Rockman Maniax*, released by Fukkan Dottokomu in 2015. During the first draft of this book, I used an informal translation prepared by Boss Fight Books Associate Editor Michael P. Williams. In February 2016, Shmuplations released an English version of this interview as "The Birth of Mega Man – 2011 Developer Interview" (http://bit.ly/20V42Z1). All quotations in this book use the publically available Shmuplations translation, though I have referred to Mike's version for those portions of the interview that Shmuplations did not translate. In addition, Mike provided a translation for the Kitamura's 2015 message to Mega Man fans not included in Shumplations's translation.

Information on the NES/Famicom hardware limitations and the way developers overcame them was sourced from *I am Error: The Nintendo Family Computer/Entertainment System Platform* by Nathan Altice (MIT Press, 2015).

Jeremy Parish's interview with composer Manami Matsumae was published as "Manami Matsumae, the Maestro of Mega Man" on January 20, 2016 at USgamer (http://bit.ly/2alud7p).

Joseph Morici's comments on *Rockman* being a "horrible title" are sourced from Richard Mitchell's article "Who Changed Rockman's Name to Mega Man" published on August 1, 2009 at Engadget (http://engt.co/2a21WGY).

Technical and historical information on NESticle came from the Nathan Altice's 2012 article "Emulate the Emulators" on Metopal (http://bit.ly/2a0OQXN) and Bloodlust Software's home page (http://bit.ly/2a22blq).

In addition to translating that Kitamura/Ariga interview for the first draft of this book, Mike also sat through hours of *Pro Yakyuu? Satsujin Jiken!* playthrough videos. The most useful of these was the 13-part Japanese-language "let's play" hosted by user Kakkashī at Niconico (http://bit.ly/2a8NzAg).

Biographical information on James Rolfe, the Angry Video Game Nerd, that didn't come directly from our interview was sourced from his 2008 video "Cinemassacre 200" (http://bit.ly/29FbC9c).

Lance Cortez and John Delia's 2012 MAGFest interview with Bryan Clark can be found on YouTube here: http://bit.ly/29Rst8K

Mohammed Taher's April 2016 interview with composer Takashi Tateishi's was published as "A Conversation with Takashi Tateishi" on Brave Wave's website (http://bit.ly/29NexOy).

Keiji Inafune's interview with Chris Hoffman of *Play Magazine* was originally published in vol. 3, issue 4 (April 2004) as "The Best Damn Mega Man Feature Period." A transcription is hosted at The Mega Man Network here: http://bit.ly/29O1tmU. Additional information about Inafune's role in the development of the Mega Man series and *Mighty No. 9* comes from "Keiji Inafune Dropped Mad Mega Man Secrets on Me" from Tony Ponce at Destructoid (http://bit.ly/2altXW0), "The Man Behind Mega Man" from Audrey Drake at IGN (http://bit.ly/29O1FST), and "Unity Exclusive: Keiji Inafune Answers Your December Mega Man Questions: Part 1" on Capcom's blog (http://bit.ly/29Rtq0E).

Artist Kiyoshi Utata's reminiscences on Akira Kitamura appeared in the Japanese fan publication *Utata Kiyoshi Art Dot Works: Interview Side*, compiled by the *dōjin* circle Gēmu Eria 51 and published by Mitsurinsha in 2011 (http://amzn.to/29TfNxd). Mike provided translations for the excerpts quoted in this book.

Quotes from Nintendo Age users come from private messages but mostly from posts on the thread "Interviewing All NA Users for a Print Book" at http://bit.ly/29Of4Nt.

Information on Inti Creates and *Mega Man 9, 10,* and the Zero spin-off series came from "Companions Through Life and Death: The Story of Inti Creates and Mega Man" by Jeremy Parish at USgamer (http://bit.ly/1PJNg9K) and Parish's review of *Mega Man 10* on 1UP (http://bit.ly/2a22Fb3).

Details on the emergence of Kickstarter, Tim Schafer, and the *Mega Man Legacy Collection* can be found in: "Tim Schafer Leaves LucasArts" by Michael Mullen on GameSpot (http://bit.ly/29GDIxx); "An Experiment Failed" by Chris Morris on CNN (http://cnnmon.ie/29NeMcy); Gamasutra's 2009 sales charting citing the low sales of *Brütal Legend* (http://ubm.io/2a01hnT); "Broken Age, the First Blockbuster Kickstarter Game, Is Finally Finished" by Zach Kotzer on Vice (http://bit.ly/1EhKL9t); and "The Most In-Depth Mega Man Legacy Collection Interview You'll Read Today" at USgamer by Jeremy Parish (http://bit.ly/29GDwOy).

•

Kurokawa

The confusion surrounding the identity of Masahiko Kurokawa a.k.a Patariro is worth a chapter in itself, but this note will have to suffice. The best source on Kurokawa is his entry at the fan wiki Striderpedia, but we set out to discover just why exactly "his work is often incorrectly attributed to 'Masayoshi Kurokawa'" (http://bit.ly/29FbQgA).

In 2009, Sam Roberts ("Scion") and Rob Strangman ("Dire51") interviewed Koichi Yotsui ("Isuke") of *Strider* (Arcade, 1989) fame, who was one of the developers who defected from Capcom along with Akira Kitamura to form the short-lived game studio Takeru. The interview was transcribed in Japanese and translated to English on the Strider series fansite Light Sword Cypher Mainframe (LSCM) as "Interview with Kouichi 'Isuke' Yotsui" (http://bit. ly/2a8OmBf), and later reprinted in English in Strangman's self-published *Memoirs of a Virtual Caveman* (2014). In this interview, Yotsui reminisces on the development of *Strider*, and the role that Masahiko Kurokawa (黒川雅彦) had in the "consumer version." The credits of this version—the NES adaptation of *Strider*—list Patariro as the game designer.

Despite Yotsui's clear connection between his colleague Masahiko Kurokawa and the psuedonym Patariro, common sources of information like Wikipedia and MobyGames (http://bit.ly/29HV3VH) nevertheless credit games like *Strider* and *Mega Man 3* to Masayoshi Kurokawa (黒川真 圭) instead. MobyGames does have a separate page (http:// bit.ly/29TgGG8) for "Masayoshi Kurokawa," whose scant credits include *Resident Evil* (1996) and its 1997 *Director's Cut*, and curiously, 1986's *Ghosts 'n Goblins*, a game whose neverending loop of gameplay leaves no room for a staff credits roll whatsover. Could there really have been a Masahiko Kurokawa working on a 1986 Capcom game, who then worked on absolutely nothing else until *Resident Evil*, while in the meantime Masayoshi Kurokawa subbed in to work on 1987's *Higemaru Makaijima: Nanatsu no Shima*

Daibōken up through 1993's *Mega Man 6*? The answer is: probably not.

Capcom, however, has officially little to say on the matter. Stephanie Palermo, Associate PR Manager at Capcom, told me by email that " [i]f you suppose he changed his name, or any other thing occurred after his work here, that sounds like it would fall under his personal life and isn't our business to speak to." Assuming he did in fact change his name (or adopt a new one), we could unify those credits at MobyGames and make the picture somewhat clearer. Throughout most of his career at Capcom, Kurokawa went by Patariro, until 1996's cinematic *Resident Evil*, which eschewed the cute arcade pseudonyms more suitable for a Mega Man game. Here, Kurokawa is credited in full as Masahiko Kurokawa, and he even appeared in person at a presentation at V Jump Festival '95 highlighting a prototype of *Resident Evil* (http:// bit.ly/29Tg3w7). But just the following year, he broke ranks with Capcom to join game studio Whoopee Camp, where he worked under the name Masayoshi Kurokawa on *Tomba!* (1997) and its sequel *Tomba! 2* (1999). After the demise of Whoopee Camp, Kurokawa worked on Deep Space's *Extermination* (2001) and *Hungry Ghosts* (2003). MobyGames additionally credits Masayoshi Kurokawa for *Deadly Premonition* (2010) and its 2013 *Director's Cut*, but this must be a different person, as Yotsui's interview with Roberts and Strangman establishes that Masahiko had already died by 2009.

The final pieces of the puzzle came from searching the web for information in Japanese. From the website Shinsekai

Gēmu Sutaffu Risuto Shinpō (a.k.a. Project - Videogame Staff Credits), we get a different picture of Kurokawa Masayoshi (http://bit.ly/2a0P5ls). This profile includes familiar facts (his famous moniker Patariro, and his earliest game as Capcom's 1986 *Commando* where he was credited as "Kuro"). It also provides new information, like how he was born in 1963 in Osaka, the city where Capcom has its headquarters, and how he eventually went on to become an game design instructor at Human Academy Co., Ltd. after leaving the world of professional game development. Another unexpected detail: He was a member of a theatrical troupe called Gekidan Neko no Mori.

In a July 22, 2008 post at his now-defunct blog Suteru Nya Oshii Sutezerifu!!!, dedicated to independent theatre in the Kansai Region in which Osaka is a major urban area, Gekidan Neko no Mori member Kazuhiko Takase laments the death of his troupemate Masayoshi Kurokawa, who he says has died at age 45—thus placing his birth in roughly 1963 (http://bit.ly/29GDR3M). A photo on this obituary, while small, also identifies as Kurokawa a person who looks not unlike the man in the V Jump *Resident Evil* video. As for the troupe itself, their website's member page includes as a special mention for Masayoshi Kurokawa, wishing him "bon voyage" (http://bit.ly/2a401ym).

With all this circumstantial evidence, we reached out to the only member of Gekidan Neko no Mori currently active on social media, Manami Nankoh. Nankoh confirmed via Twitter that the Masahiko Kurokawa in the *Resident Evil* presentation video from 1995 was indeed her troupe's

Masayoshi Kurokawa. She remembered he had had a career in games and said that "Masayoshi" was his stage name. Writing fondly of Kurokawa, Nankoh told Mike unambiguously: "*Kurokawa Masahiko-san wa Kurokawa Masayoshi-san desu.*" Masahiko is Masayoshi.

Whether or not Capcom's PR folks were aware of Kurokawa's theatrical penchant for using multiple names is up for debate, but the identity of Patariro is no longer a mystery.

ACKNOWLEDGEMENTS

First, thanks to Theresa Beckhusen whose support and love make everything I do possible. You've endured countless basketball games, wrestling promos, and trips to game stores and flea markets for obscure Famicom titles. I admire you, I'm humbled by you, and I'm honored you share your life with me.

Thanks to Gabe Durham who patiently guided this book from a vague project about *Panic Restaurant* into its final, truest form. You've handled your share of scattered, frenzied emails, and everything you've done with Boss Fight is so important for the games community.

Thanks especially to Michael P. Williams for researching and translating much of the material that constructed the historical core of this book. Your research into Masahiko Kurokawa and *Professional Baseball? Murder Case!* was absolutely essential, and I can't tell you enough how grateful I am you once spent hours on a

Saturday morning explaining to me the nuances of a never-before-translated Akira Kitamura interview.

Thank you to Talia Nadir, the Research and Instruction Librarian at my home institution, the University of St. Thomas, for acquiring multiple books for this project and collaborating with Michael P. Williams at the University of Pennsylvania. Your enthusiasm and determination truly helped this manuscript during a very critical point.

Thanks to Alyse Knorr for reading an early draft of this book and providing detailed, constructive feedback.

Thanks to Ken Baumann for not only the gorgeous cover and book design, but for writing *Earthbound*—a book that influenced much of my thinking on *Mega Man 3*.

Thanks to Joseph M. Owens, Nick Sweeney, Ryan Plummer—my former student(!)—for proofreading this manuscript and digging out my typos and redundancies.

Thanks to James Rolfe, the Angry Video Game Nerd, for agreeing to be interviewed about his career and Mega Man and for the hundreds of hours of entertainment that made me feel like I wasn't alone.

Thanks to Justin Heckert for keeping me interested in retro gaming and traveling all over the country with me to look for obscure NES games nobody wants to play.

Thanks to Akira "AK" Kitamura, Keiji "Inafking" Inafune, Masahiko "Patariro" Kurokawa, and all the unsung heroes of not just Capcom but all the Japanese game studios that defined a generation and a medium.

Thanks to the University of St. Thomas for providing me funding and time to present my work on *Mega Man 3*, collaboration, and translation at NonfictionNow 2015.

Thanks to the Digital Humanities Summer Institute and especially to Andy Keenan and Matt Bouchard, instructors of the Games for Digital Humanists class that appears in this book. You both complicated my thinking about game criticism at a critical juncture in the development of this project.

Thank you to my parents for always supporting me and my writing and encouraging me to leave Scranton and pursue my education. More importantly, thanks for buying me an NES in 1989 and patiently sitting through ten thousand hours of me rambling about video games.

Thanks to Mike Meoni and RJ Boose for introducing me to NESticle, Sega Saturn, and a whole lot more. Your memories live on.

SPECIAL THANKS

For making our third season of books possible, Boss Fight Books would like to thank Maxwell Neely-Cohen, Cathy Durham, Edwin Locke, Mark Kuchler, Ken Durham, alraz, Adam B Wenzel, Sam Grawe, Jared Wadsworth, Sean Flannigan, Angus Fletcher, Patrick Tenney, Joshua Mallory, Brit W., Tomio Ueda, Joel Bergman, Sunjay Kelkar, Joe Murray, David Hayes, and Shawn Reed.

ALSO FROM
BOSS FIGHT BOOKS